CROSSING LINES

CROSSING LINES

RACE AND MIXED RACE

ACROSS THE GEOHISTORICAL DIVIDE

EDITED BY

Marc Coronado
Rudy P. Guevarra, Jr.
Jeffrey Moniz
Laura Furlan Szanto

Multiethnic Student Outreach
University of California, Santa Barbara

To purchase copies, please contact
the Center for Chicano Studies,
University of California, Santa Barbara.

PRINTED IN
THE UNITED STATES OF AMERICA

Cover Illustration
Crossing Lines, by Jeffrey Moniz and Rudy P. Guevarra, Jr.

Book Design
Laura Furlan Szanto

Book Production
Sasha Briar Newborn/Sabine Design

Multiethnic Student Outreach (MESO)
in collaboration with
the Center for Chicano Studies
at the University of California, Santa Barbara.

ISBN 0-9700384-1-0

ACKNOWLEDGMENTS

Crossing Lines, both the April 2002 student/faculty conference at UCSB and the book you hold in your hands, would not have been possible without the help, encouragement, and guidance of many, many people. The editors would like to thank those who enabled our vision of a multidisciplinary forum for the discussion of race and mixed race.

First, we must thank our families for their inspiration and their enduring patience. For many of us, forging a space for the discussion of race and multiracial identity is something we deal with daily, both inside and outside the academy. The people we love give our work meaning. We thank them for their continued support, their willingness to listen to us rant, and their courage to live life on their own terms (often in spite of us, their over-intellectualizing parents, children, siblings, and partners).

We also want to acknowledge the University of California faculty who treated us as colleagues with meaningful work to do. Each of them has been a leader in contemporary academic discussions about race, and all have been instrumental in the success of our particular project. They include, from UCSB: Paul Spickard, History professor and mentor to most of us; Carl Gutierrez-Jones, chair of the English Department, interim-chair of the Center for Chicano Studies, and stalwart ally to Multiethnic Student Outreach; G. Reginald (Reg) Daniel, assistant professor of Sociology and inspirational social activist; Kip Fulbeck, professor in the Art Studio Department, artist, performer, and provocateur; and María Herrera-Sobek, Chair of the Department of Chicano Studies, Acting Associate Vice Chancellor for Academic Policy, and compassionate friend. George Lipsitz, professor of Ethnic Studies and director of the Thurgood Marshall Institute and the San Diego Social Science History Project at UCSD, agreed to be the keynote speaker for our 2002 conference when Crossing Lines was merely a dream, shared among friends. His integrity, his passion, and his generosity have made our project a success beyond all expectation.

Funding for the publication of these proceedings was provided by grants from UCSB Chancellor Henry T. Yang, Vice

6

Chancellor of Student Affairs Michael D. Young, the Rockefeller Foundation, and the Office of Research. The majority of our funding was provided by the Center for Chicano Studies at UCSB, which has a proud history of committment to both scholarship and the community. The staff of the Center, and Anne Elwell in particular, made us all feel like we knew what we were doing even when we clearly did not.

Crossing Lines began as a conference, designed and organized by students, and we would like to thank all of the organizations and departments, volunteers, graduate students, undergrads, faculty and staff who made that event possible and who encouraged us to publish our papers. Finally, we must thank our own students, whose wisdom and whose questions keep us thinking and working, and to whom we are forever grateful.

The Editors

TABLE OF CONTENTS

Introduction   9

Clueless
  Rudy P. Guevarra, Jr.   15

Noises in the Blood: Culture, Conflict, and
Mixed Race Identities
  George Lipsitz   19

Does Multiraciality Lighten? Me-Too Ethnicity and
the Whiteness Trap
  Paul Spickard   45

"My Father? Gabacho?" Ethnic Doubling in
Gloria Lopez Stafford's *A Place in El Paso*
  Marc Coronado   63

Burritos and Bagoong: Mexipinos and Multiethnic
Identity in San Diego, California
  Rudy P. Guevarra, Jr.   73

Challenging the Hegemony of Multiculturalism:
The Matter of the Marginalized Multiethnic
  Jeffrey A. S. Moniz   97

Beyond Disobedience
  Nicole M. Williams   117

"Fictive Imaginings": Constructing Biracial Identity
and Senna's *Caucasia*
  Carina A. Evans   135

The Beginning
  Laura Furlan Szanto   149

Los Angeles Museum of Art: Looking Forward
    Melinda Gándara   151

Multiethnic Mexican Americans in Demographic
and Ethnographic Perspectives
    Tomás R. Jiménez   161

Contributors   190

INTRODUCTION

Those of us who work in multiracial studies often ask ourselves whether or not we're helping the cause of social justice when we emphasize the multiple overlaps and focus on the crossing lines of culture, race, and ethnicity that exist among various ethnic groups. We wonder if we simply muddy the waters of ethnic studies when we enlarge conversations about race and racism with the concerns of multiracial people. We fear that we may play into the erasure that is colorblindness when we emphasize our commonalities across racial or ethnic lines rather than focus on our bonds with specific ethnic groups. We worry that there may be more real power available to racialized peoples and more real peace possible if we work instead to sustain ethnic and racial nationalism. These are the concerns that provoked us to write and compile the articles for *Crossing Lines*. Certainly, scholars and social activists have spent a considerable amount of time carving out spaces inside and outside the academy for the discussions of race in the U.S. But even with all our doubts, we believed that by crossing established academic disciplinary lines and by crossing the territorial lines that too often limit studies of ethnicity among members of the academy we might make the discussion more reflective of true, lived human experience.

In the spring of 2000, graduate students at UCSB who were working in history, education, English, sociology, and the arts came together to form Multiethnic Student Outreach. Our primary cause was recruiting and enrolling a more diverse graduate student population for our university. We traveled across the country to talk to undergraduates about attending UCSB, and as we became friends, we inevitably began to discuss our own research. It didn't take long to realize that all of us shared an interest in the intersections of our disciplines, and that as we shared information across disciplinary lines our own work became more nuanced and honest. We also shared a common concern for the inheritors of traditions of struggle represented by the multiple ethnic groups we were writing about and working with. This book is the result of our conversations, our own independent studies, and the Crossing Lines conference held in April 2002 on the UCSB Campus.

GEORGE LIPSITZ's passionate keynote address to that conference opens our discussion by asking about the future of mixed-race consciousness and political mobilization. He notes that race may have been historically represented as "noises in the blood and echoes in the bone," but that race is also a part of lived realities. Seldom do racialized groups consider their own members part of a homogeneous whole, but they are often willing to portray themselves in this way if it can serve as a means of creating or sustaining political solidarity. For some, however, this sort of essentializing strategy is not enough. Lipsitz points to the "great personal pain and considerable political disempowerment" that those who choose mixed-race identity risk by refusing to be pigeon-holed, and to the promise that a combination of political strategies may provide for all people. He asserts that "drawing on bloodlines of belief and act[ing] in arenas not determined by their skin color or phenotype may hold the key to formulating a politics of mixed-race identity." His vision is that this crossing and re-crossing of ethnic lines, which Lipsitz refers to as "strategic anti-essentialism and branching out," may enable a panethnic collectivity led by multiracial consciousness.

PAUL SPICKARD considers similar issues of ethnic fluidity or choice in his comparison of Whiteness and Multiracial studies. In the article that his generous editors and the kind folks at Sage Publications allowed us to reprint here, he looks at the "constructivist concept of ethnicity" on which both intellectual projects depend, and at the critical claims that both concepts depend on the idea of racial erasure or "Whitening." Ultimately, he argues that acceptance of the plasticity of race or ethnicity enables multiracial individuals to subvert the "Whiteness trap" by embracing all of the various aspects of their background. Through the use of historical examples, he points out how racial boundaries become less rigid and multiracial people can retain links to communities of color even as they claim their multiracial identities. The vital issue here is not which ethnic group do multiracial people choose, but how they maintain their links to communities of color if they choose to identify as multiracial.

I'm MARC CORONADO, and I pick up these questions of community loyalty as I analyze a contemporary American memoir, *A Place in El Paso*, written by Gloria Lopez Stafford. My work asks what personal attributes are necessary to sustain a multivalent racial or ethnic choice. Making such a choice is seldom easy. It often alienates the people we need most—those in our own family or neighborhood. Psychological flexibility and a willingness to be compassionate to those who don't quite understand such decisions seem to be the most pronounced qualities that Lopez Stafford's memoir puts forward. Too often personal rigidity results from a legacy of racial oppression, and its limits and inflexibility haunt its victims. Ultimately, this paralysis limits our ability to fully integrate the two worlds that border dwellers must live in. An effective multiethnic community comes at the price of constant nurturing, educating, building, and rebuilding.

RUDY P. GUEVARRA, JR.'s work takes us into just such an ethnically blended Mexipino community in San Diego, California. Through his remarkable collection of oral histories, he reveals the humor, pain, and multiple connections shared by Mexicans and Filipinos in communities where intermarriage between the two groups goes back several generations. He notes that similar legacies of "immigration and wage labor experiences, community formation and a shared Spanish colonial past" laid the foundation for the bond between the two groups. He also comments on the continuing links—geographic proximity, similar religious and cultural practices, and the continuing oppression of both communities—that have given rise to generations of people who ally with both groups. He points out, however, that such mixing is not without its problems, and that even within the group, phenotype plays a role in who is accepted or rejected. "Love of family" is the underlying basis for sustaining Mexipino identity and for enabling what he calls "a new way in which to see the world."

JEFFREY MONIZ questions the older, multiculturalist way of seeing the world in his challenge to what we generally understand as cultural pluralism and multicultural education. Although multiculturalism has made significant progress in challenging White patriarchal hegemony, he argues that it in itself is also hegemonic. "Multiculturalists," he writes, "in their aspiration to assert diverse perspectives, often fail to consider those of mixed race and mixed ethnicity." Mixed folks don't fit neatly into academic boxes, and the story of multiracial people is seldom a part of the multicultural curriculum. His critique aims to transform the project, and to encourage educators to be more radically inclusive, more radically multicultural, and to radically "extend the boundaries of diversity." He argues that we must "build on the best of multiculturalism and multicultural education, yet transform [them] in a more democratic and egalitarian manner." Creating consciousness about issues of multiethnicity and multiraciality may be the place to begin.

NICOLE M. WILLIAMS' study of students at Sidelines Junior High highlights the immediacy of Jeffrey Moniz's admonition. As both authors point out, we need to recognize that ethnic difference runs deeper than multicultural pedagogy has so far led us to believe. Williams disrupts the general common perception that the teacher is "in complete control of the classroom" and acknowledges the power of oppositional subcultures to construct the classroom environment through their disruptive, or "oppositional," behaviors. The students she writes about might be called Chicano or Latino by those who don't understand the complete dynamic of their situation. But to themselves they are marginalized from even this already marginalized group. Subcultures most often set themselves apart by their construction of a new culture, at odds with the general cultural goals of their own ethnic group as well as those of the dominant ethnic group. Yet individuals in these groups create a new sense of allegiance to those who are the most marginalized in the classroom. As academics, we know that nothing is taught if nothing is learned. What Williams suggests is that we acknowledge students' desire to succeed, and recognize that they fulfill the social need to do so as part of a group. Simply labeling the manifestation of oppositional identity in a marginalized ethnic group as "disobedience" is equivalent to an abdication of the school's responsibility to educate all students.

CARINA EVANS builds on these issues of pedagogy and oppositional culture by examining the history of racializing literatures in the U.S. She asks, "What makes a black text *black*?" and then begins to unravel the ways that particular texts have called for particular readings, most significantly that of the tragic mulatto masterplot. She argues that Danzy Senna's contemporary novel *Caucasia* constructs a "new sense of biracial identity— new in that it aggressively takes on the vestiges of the old." In Evans's reading, Senna's novel undermines classic conventions of multiracial literature by opening up serious issues like racial passing to a more nuanced sense of play, reinterpretation, and subversion. Finally, she asserts that the contemporary multiracial novel's potential lies "not in the idea of racial transcendence, which fits the melting pot idea of racial utopia, but in drawing attention to the fragility of racial categories." Indeed, such a realization might enable us to generate more original and meaningful ideas about the complexities of racial identity.

LAURA FURLAN SZANTO's poignant personal narrative focuses on her attempt to determine ethnic authenticity when only fragments of the past are available to her. This search for identity is fueled by her desire to belong to an ancestral community. She writes that she occupies a "strange place between being and not being, out and in, white and red," acknowledging that culture and family often share the stage with biology and blood when we try to determine who we really are. Szanto's search for material clues that would connect her to her American Indian heritage reminds us of the damage done by centuries of our disrespect for and neglect of cultures other than the dominant one.

MELINDA GÁNDARA takes up the issue of how the material past is preserved and presented to the public in her review of the Los Angeles County Museum of Art's continuing commitment to the people of the area. She writes that in a geographic area where "Latinos already constitute and absolute majority," the traditional museum demographic is changing, and the museum is attempting to respond. If the mission of a museum is public education, preservation, and presentation of the material life of the community, Gándara feels that LACMA is well-positioned to serve these needs "regardless of whose California and which California it turns out to be." Reterritorialization is taking place all across the American Southwest as the demographics of the area shift.

TOMÁS JIMÉNEZ takes a close look at "whose California" Mexican American children are growing up in today. His work examines the ethnic identity of the offspring of Mexican/White intermarriages, using both U.S. Census data and in-depth interviews with multiethnic Mexican Americans in California. Census data indicates that these children are most often given "a Mexican label much more often than they are given a white non-Hispanic label by others." However, his interviews indicate that these same individuals most often assert a Mexican American, or blended, ethnic identity themselves. Even as they do so, they confront ethnic boundaries and sharp divisions between ethnic categories that influence the extent to which they feel free to assert any one particular identity.

As each of the writers in this collection argues, crossing ethnic lines is never a simple act. Such border crossing calls on the individual to dig deeply to understand the self as well as her place in the community and the collective. It demands compassion and patience for and from family and friends, strength of character in the face of racism, and a willingness to fight for individual and collective rights. Such crossing calls on our communities to reassess our basis for inclusion as well as our ability to embrace diversity and change. Perhaps most importantly, such crossing of racial and ethnic lines encourages the building of meaningful collectivity, enriched by the recognition of difference and empowered by multiplicity.

Marc Coronado

A Note on the Design of Crossing Lines:

Readers will notice that APA, Chicago, and MLA (and even a few hybrid) styles are represented in *Crossing Lines.* This stylistic choice underscores our multidisciplinary collaboration, and we hope it will encourage work across disciplinary lines. Academic miscegenation can empower our research and extend the possibilities of our lives.

Rudy P. Guevarra, Jr., Jeffrey Moniz, and Laura Furlan Szanto are responsible for the beauty of this book. Rudy and Jeff designed the Crossing Lines logo depicting people embracing each other and our globe. Jeff designed the MESO logo, inspired he says by an owl who visited his patio as he worked. Laura took the raw material from ten different authors and turned our ideas into a book, caring about every detail and working her artistic magic on every page.

CLUELESS

RUDY P. GUEVARRA, JR.

UNIVERSITY OF CALIFORNIA, SANTA BARBARA

What's it like to be me, you ask?
Better yet,
What are you?
So many times I hear this phrase
For those who don't know what I am
But for those who think they have a clue
You assume,
That I'm what you perceive me to be
But it's not what I see in my reflection,
Not what I see when I look at my mother,
My father
I'm the product, the offspring,
The creation of two worlds
Now into one beating heart,
One soul with one desire to be seen
Don't look at my goatee,
My baggy jeans,
My short combed back hair,
Or even my head when I rock a pelon
My skin color can be deceiving
Unless you've painted my picture for me
I'm not the brown unknown,
But a Filipino dragon flying high up in the clouds
I'm the ancient serpent of pre-Columbian
cultures,
Among the warriors of the inner cities and
yuppies of the suburbs
I am your illusion, your reality, your future
Mestizo you call me,
But what the hell is that?
Does that include all of me?
My Asian, Indian, African, and Spanish roots?

Can you see my multidimensional character?
　　The complexity of my being, my existence,
　　　　Which thrives on the ignorance of the masses
I am the Filipino you despised, the one you hated,
　　The Mexican you abhorred, ignore, and continue to attack
　　　　　　　But wait...What if I was both?
Could you deal with the double reality of my presence?
What am I you say?
　　What's it like to be me?
　　　　A multiethnic individual of the twenty-first century
　　　　　　A creation of two similar cultures, yet very
　　　　　　　　different histories
I am a Mexipino
Mexican by birth, by land, by blood
　　Filipino in the same right and with the utmost pride
　　I may not be your typical Pinoy,
　　　　Your typical Chicano,
　　　　　　But I am one among the many,
　　　　　　　　So deal with it.
I may be foreign to you,
　　Exotic, even threatening,
　　　　But so many times I can be invisible too
My illusion masks my inner thoughts, but not what I see
　　And it sure as hell won't cloud my sanity
　　　　I know who I am.
See my genetic, cultural, social, and political identity,
　　Is often in question but it's all the same to me,
　　　　I'm the multiple mestizo
　　　　　　if you can call me such a thing
From the shores of the Philippines, my ancestors call,
　　Sending messages from Cavite, Pangasinan
　　　　Land of my forefathers,
　　　　　　Lest I not forget
Blending in the whirlwinds of the Americas,
　　Touching down unnoticed, dancing,
In Michoacán,
　　Purépero my grandfather says,
　　　　Lest I not forget
Let the voices of my ancestors carry me,
　　Into the cradle of my country

America ...
But what am I, you ask?
What's it like to be me?
If you don't already know,
Then I can't help you
Because I already gave you
The clue that passed you by.

NOISES IN THE BLOOD: CULTURE, CONFLICT, AND MIXED RACE IDENTITIES

GEORGE LIPSITZ

UNIVERSITY OF CALIFORNIA, SAN DIEGO

> To get anywhere in life you have to follow a
> road....To make anything happen, you have
> to walk through the crossroads.
>
> — Moris Moriset[1]

In our society where opportunities and life chances are systematically skewed along racial lines, where housing segregation and racial profiling routinely relegate people of different races to different physical and social spaces, the rule of race often remains unchallenged and unquestioned. Racial segregation is so pervasive that it comes to seem natural, necessary, and inevitable. Under these circumstances, race provides protective cover for widespread injustice and inequality. As W. E. B. Du Bois demonstrated in *Black Reconstruction in America*, racism makes it easy for people with privilege "to discount and misunderstand the suffering or harm done to others." Du Bois noted that "all consciousness of inflicting ill disappears" once degradation and exploitation are "hidden beneath a different color of skin."[2] Desperate poverty, onerous labor, poor health, and inadequate shelter come to be seen as the personal qualities of particular aggrieved groups rather than results of exploitation and exclusion.

Among people who identify themselves (or who are identified by others) as "mixed race," however, the artifice of race is often visible, self-evident, and even inescapable. People whose families include members of different races can rarely take race for granted. If for no other reason than self-defense, they need to learn the nature of the racial regimes that they and their relatives are certain to encounter in even the most casual social interactions. Under the best of circumstances, mixed race identity can provide a useful optic on power, a privileged standpoint from which important aspects of social relations can be absorbed, analyzed, and understood.

Yet mixed race identity can also be a source of great personal pain and considerable political disempowerment. Of course, *all* people are mixed race because pure races do not exist. The history of humans has been a history of intermixing.[3] But even among those who recognize that *all* identities are socially constructed, that all ethnic groups are coalitions, and that racial identities are political, provisional, and strategic constructions rather than biological or anthropological facts, mixed race people can sometimes find themselves unwanted in any group, ridiculed as disloyal, despised as the "other's other," because they carry within their embodied selves an identity that seems to threaten the unity and uniformity of aggrieved collectivities. It does not help that this is an identity that can even be something of a mystery to those identified by it. "I think I must be a mixed blood," confides Cherokee artist Jimmie Durham, seemingly referring to the vexed question of how much Indian ancestry is required to designate any individual as a true Native American. But then, with a joke that calls into question the very categories that cause controversy, Durham notes, "I claim to be male, although only one of my parents was male."[4]

One difficulty that mixed race people confront comes from the strong solidarity that has been built within and among aggrieved racial groups through metaphorical and metonymic references to biology, to common bloodlines and bones. In her brilliant analysis of gender, orality, and vulgarity in Jamaican culture, Carolyn Cooper points to "the metonymy of blood and bone" embedded in novelist Vic Reid's definition of a true Griot. Ordinary storytellers can get their wisdom from anywhere, Reid's narrator tells us in Nanny Town, but the knowledge of a Griot comes from deep inside, "like an echo in the bone or a noise in the blood."[5]

Artists, intellectuals, and activists working within antiracist contexts have often made much of these noises and echoes. A strong and evocative tradition appealing to embodiment and ancestry has been an important form of self-defense for members of aggrieved communities. Black nationalism, *Chicanismo*, the American Indian Movement, separatist feminism, and many other forms of identity-based mobilization have made permanent and enduring contributions to the struggle for social justice. Because social inequality is so often inscribed on the body, solidarity based on skin color, phenotype, and sex, on shared experiences or shared ancestry, has functioned frequently as a means of turning hegemony on its head, a way to transform negative ascription into positive affirmation, and a vehicle for building identification with a common "we" instead of an isolated "me." Yet appeals to blood and bone have ultimately proved themselves unreliable and unsuccessful. They privilege biology over belief, and promise more sameness than any group's experiences can actually sustain. By emphasizing the identity of the victim rather than the innate injustices of victimization, movements based solely on identity can encourage each group to seek gains at the expense of others, to settle for "new faces in high places" rather than using the knowledge that all oppressed groups have about the necessity to challenge all exploitation, dehumanization, and injustice.[6]

Because of the history of identity-based solidarity within aggrieved racial groups, it is understandable that mixed race people might feel tempted to fashion a firm and fixed identity category out of their diverse experiences. Embodiment and ancestry seem to determine the social status of mixed race people and consequently they might serve as important symbols in the struggle. Yet symbolism is not substance. A closer look at the experiences of "raced" people in struggles for social justice reveals that reliance on firm and fixed identities has been more apparent than real. Even the most militant forms of nationalism have never assumed that all members of an aggrieved group are alike. On the contrary, nationalist movements have characteristically struggled to graft clear political meanings onto diffuse group identities, often devoting much more time to changing ideas and attitudes within their own groups than battling those outside.

By promoting the term "Chicano," Mexican American activists of the 1960s and 1970s sought a political rather than a biological source of self-definition. The term "Chicano" guided them to build egalitarian solidarity around the needs of the most despised and oppressed part of their community, to disrupt the U.S. "ethnic" model of assimilation through deracination by evoking the mythical Aztlán, a nation that could not be unproblematically absorbed into national projects of either the United States or Mexico. Chicano militants attempted to build a common political project for a community that they recognized as deeply divided by region and religion, by language and legal status, by gender and generation. Similarly, the Asian American movement built a new collective U.S. panethnic identity among people with a wide range of class positions, people whose ancestors came from many different national backgrounds, spoke different languages, and practiced distinctly different religions.

What we now remember as nationalist identity-based struggles were often in fact recognitions of inter-cultural and inter-ethnic connections. In a revealing reflection, Chicano scholar-activist Carlos Muñoz recalls, "When we started the movement in the '60s, we tried to redefine ourselves as a mixed-race people of color both Spanish and Indian. Then, as we developed Chicano Studies, we discovered that African slaves were also taken throughout Mexico and elsewhere in the Americas, in the Vera Cruz and Acapulco areas in particular. We discovered that Asians were also taken to Mexico and Latin America. For example, the Spanish at one time brought Filipino slaves to Mexico."[7] Attorney, activist, and cultural worker Chris Iijima remembers the construction of Asian American identity as a means to an end, not an end in itself. "It was created as an organizing tool to mobilize Asians to participate in the progressive movements of the times," Iijima asserts. "It was as much a mechanism to identify with one another as to identify with the struggles of others whether it is African Americans or Asians overseas, and that it was less a marker of what one was and more a marker of what one believed," he concludes.[8]

Decisions about the present and future of mixed race consciousness and political affiliation need to be made with a full understanding of the figurative meaning of embodiment and ancestry within the "race-based" tradition of social justice struggles. What seem on the surface like essentialist appeals to embodiment and ancestry often turn out, on closer inspection, to be figurative ways of locating people in the present as the inheritors of historical traditions of struggle, suffering, sacrifice, and success, not as people with unmediated and unproblematic access to noises in the blood and echoes in the bone. The great Oneida poet Roberta Hill tells us about echoes she feels in her bones in "Preguntas." In the poem she describes her literature professor, a political refugee from Chile, who tells Hill, "Your bones contain your people's history." She discovers a seemingly literal (rather than figurative) dimension to his statement when she visits her home state and learns that "there is a bounty for brown women like me." Instead of the usual announcements for "turkey shoots"—competitions in which sharp shooters vie for prize Thanksgiving turkeys as rewards for marksmanship, Hill finds a sign at a local pizzeria in Medford, Wisconsin, that vents Anti-Indian hatred by proclaiming "The First Annual Indian Shoot." Hill writes, "I felt the bones in my fingers and I scruffed them across the sign. " 'It is not the first,' the right fingerbones sang. 'It has never been annual,' the left ones added."[9]

Hill's bones speak directly to her in this poem. They testify to the horrors of history and their continuing legacy in the present. But the "wisdom" in Hill's bones is activated, informed, and augmented by the experiences that her Chilean teacher had with political repression in South America. Hill connects the lessons she learned early in life from her father's "singing" and "sobbing," from "his struggle against the daily snare of being declared worthless" to the "cloud of loneliness and loss, of solidarity with those who suffer" that she sees on her professor's face. She expresses gratitude to her teacher, because the resemblance between her suffering and his teaches a larger lesson. Her suffering is not her peculiar and particular burden, but rather part of a broader context of injustice, not just a personal inheritance. It has more to do with the sickness of her enemies than with any deficiencies in her. "You have helped me understand," she tells her teacher, "their fear of the dark is not my identity."[10]

Within aggrieved racialized communities, dancing has often been figured as a means of summoning up the ancestral presence. Through collective ritual, dancers' bodies seem to remember what the mind may have forgotten. Haitian vodou and Rara ceremonies directly seek communication with the ancestors. The ring shout serves as a constantly renewable source of moral instruction and solidarity for African Americans.[11]

Participants in Danza Azteca collectives burn sage and re-enact ancient dances to locate themselves within a long tradition of indigenous and Mexican artistry and religious belief.[12] Pilipino Cultural Nights on college campuses salute their ancestors by presenting elaborate production numbers organized around kalapati, binasuan, tinikling, and other folk dances of the Philippines. From the Ghost Dance to the Grass Dance, many instances of American Indian cultural revival and ethnic renewal have revolved around embodied activities that make ethnic identification a physical as well as an ideological process.[13] Yet dancing like this creates the very solidarity it invokes. Although seemingly speaking to the past and the ancestors, these ritual performances also call a community into being through performance, staging a solidarity in the present capable of pointing the way toward the future. The active process of coordinated and collective movement inscribes in the body the very messages it purports to find there, it creates a past capable of serving the present by using the imagined solidarity of the past as a guideline for the present and the future.

It is not that noises in the blood and echoes in the bone do not exist. The true Griots in Jamaica that Vic Reid celebrates hear the same sounds that W. E. B. Du Bois detected in the spiritual "sorrow songs" that, he said, "stirred me strangely," even though he did not know the meaning of the words they contained. But the words simply served as place markers for a deeper shared historical experience. Du Bois explains that these inchoate words and ancient melodies came from his grandmother's grandmother "who was seized by an evil Dutch trader two centuries ago." She sang her song to her child and "the child sang it to his children and they to their children's children, and so two hundred years it has traveled down to us and we sing it to our children, knowing as little as our fathers what its words may mean, but knowing well the meaning of its music."[14] Frederick Douglass heard those noises in the blood in songs that seemed to him made up of "unmeaning jargon, but which, nevertheless, were full of meaning to themselves."[15] For Tongva artist L. Frank and Chinese American writer Nellie Wong noises in the blood are also heard literally as well as figuratively. "Sometimes when I'm working with soapstone, I can hear the voices of the ancestors," says Frank.[16] Wong contends that in order to begin writing her story she had to "reach deep into the voices of the past of my ancestors, the women I saw as warriors: Li Ching Chao, Wu Tsao, Chiu Chin, and the unknown women of my parents' ancestral village in Toishan, in Guangzhaou, China...."[17]

Contact with ancestors can inform, authorize, and empower artists, intellectuals, and activists in the present. "I come from a long line of eloquent illiterates whose history reveals what words don't say," explains Chicana poet Lorna Dee Cervantes.[18] Farah Jasmine Griffin shows that the "ancestor" figure in Black fiction functions to remind readers of the strength and sustenance they can draw from the past. In the writings of Toni Morrison, Griffin notes, fiction itself can serve as a surrogate for actual ancestors.[19] Bahamian poet Marion Bethel's tribute to the feminist activist group DAWN positions politics in the present as a partial means of paying debts to the past. Her poem "And the Trees Still Stand" addresses ancestors directly, proclaiming that "we" are here because "you" made a road for us, beating back the bush, raking rocks and stones, pitched scalded tar, and uprooted trees "to turn that unchartered road into a journey with landmarks."[20]

However much we recognize that these metaphors and metonyms are constructed, fabricated, and strategically deployed, we must also recognize that their power to mobilize a solidarity based on sameness has been an important marker of identity within anti-racist struggle. And it is precisely this solidarity through sameness that seems denied to people identified or identifying themselves as mixed race.

What do echoes in the bones and noises in the blood mean to mixed race people? What can they mean to former Black Panther Johnny Spain, who felt that he had to keep secret his mother's white identity in order to be part of the Black struggle?[21] What can they mean to UC Berkeley Ethnic Studies Professor Tiya Miles, some of whose Cherokee ancestors likely owned some of her Black slave ancestors? What can they mean to Marie and Anita Daulne of the music group Zap Mama, two sisters whose Belgian father was killed by Congolese revolutionaries in that nation's war for independence, and whose politically suspect status forced their Congolese mother to flee the country with them and migrate to Belgium? What can echoes in the bone and noises in the blood mean to the 600,000 Asian Americans who are also Latino, to the 1.7 million Latinos who are also Black, to the 93.6 percent of the people who claim Native American ancestry yet report their race to be white?[22]

Exactly which noises and which echoes resonate for Cape Verde Islanders, whose ancestors are both Portuguese and African; for Lumbees, whose ancestors are white, Black, and Native American; or for Garifunas, whose ancestors were Blacks but not slaves, Indians but not North American, citizens of Belize, but also Honduras, Guatemala, and the United States, and "native" speakers of English, Spanish, and Garifuna?

The unease that these questions provoke among mixed race people hold enormous import at the present moment, because neo-liberal and neo-conservative opportunists seeking to undermine enforcement of U.S. civil rights laws see the existence of mixed race people as a strategic wedge that might be used to reject claims for social justice from aggrieved racial groups. In order to evade their responsibilities to communities of color for the continuing effects of the unfair gains and unjust enrichments generated by past and present discrimination, neo-liberals and neo-conservatives alike seize on the existence of mixed race people as a means of representing race in the U.S. as personal, private, individual, and idiosyncratic rather than institutional, ideological, collective, and cumulative. They hope that a proliferation of new identities will fragment the solidarity of aggrieved groups and frustrate race-based remedies for discrimination like affirmative action. If racial identities are uncertain and racial boundaries unclear, then the privileges of white supremacy can be secured and the manifestly racial injuries suffered by the victims of discrimination in housing and employment, from mortgage and insurance redlining, from racial profiling, and environmental racism will not be remedied. Although these provocateurs generally demonstrate no sincere interest in, and no actual knowledge about, the experiences, problems, or perspectives of mixed race people, they nonetheless see great tactical utility in the mixed race category. As David Parker and Miri Song warn us, "The topic of 'mixed race' can bring out the worst in people."[23]

Deliberately confusing a desire for recognition with a renunciation of rights, neo-conservative UC Regent Ward Connerly argues that the successful effort to allow individuals to check more than one racial category on the 2000 census form represents "a protracted outcry over the census's focus on race." Neo-liberal UC Berkeley historian David Hollinger argues that mixed race people are now performing a valuable service to American society by making ethno-racial affiliation a matter of individual choice and preference rather than a matter of external or institutional ascription. "It is the willingness to form new communities rather than merely remaining loyal to old ones," Hollinger argues, that distinguishes mixed race people as "worthy" in comparison with the disreputable raced subjects that Hollinger rejects who remain "loyal" to "old" racial categories that no longer have determinate meaning in his eyes.[24]

Yet Hollinger makes it clear that the voluntary choice made by mixed race people must be the one that *he* has chosen for them. As George Sanchez points out in his devastating critique of the fantasy of "mixed race" identity as the cost-free solution to the racial ills of the U.S., Hollinger's argument is racist because it is based on biology, alleging that it is the mixed gene pools of mixed race people that force them to choose a mixed race identity. Hollinger's argument is also totalitarian because his formulation allows mixed race people to identify only as mixed race. For Hollinger, if they choose a white identity, they reinforce white supremacy, but if they identify completely with an aggrieved community of color, they re-inscribe the "ethnic nationalism" that Hollinger despises. To satisfy him, mixed race people must choose a dual existence, must serve as bridges between cultures and colors. As Sanchez astutely notes, "What a burden for these super-Americans to shoulder! What an abandonment of responsibility by those of us who appear to be bound by one racial identity!"[25]

Connerly and Hollinger are so eager to make race—and especially blackness—disappear, that they do not even bother to investigate the history of societies like Brazil, where the elimination of overt racial categories in law make them even more powerful as factors shaping opportunities and life chances.[26] They do not notice that allowing people to check more than one racial classification on the census entails *more* emphasis on race rather than less. As Liz Guillen of the Mexican American Legal Defense and Education Fund argues, "the fact that so many people checked the mixed race box signifies a cry for the census to capture who I really am, not to ignore race completely."[27] Connerly and Hollinger know so little about the history of ethnogenesis in the U.S. that they fail to discern that social movements for justice along racial lines have never been based in solely in biology, but rather in collective and deliberate efforts to build new communities by giving an internal political meaning to external ascription. Hollinger, in particular, is so eager to evade the overwhelming evidence that shows the salience of race in determining opportunities and life chances, that he portrays the radical solidarity of Blacks in fighting against contemporary discrimination and exclusion as merely an outdated loyalty to a "past" community.

What were the architects of Asian American and Native American panethnicity doing in the 1960s and 1970s if not creating new voluntary communities based on shared intellectual and cultural understandings? What were the advocates of *Chicanismo* and Black Power doing if not giving a political definition to a presumed biological identity and then striving to persuade others in their groups to adopt those politics? As Alexandra Harmon emphasizes in discussing Native American ethnogenesis, "virtually every characteristic or practice that has marked Indians in the past—name, physical appearance, language, location, method of governance, religion, kinship system, and even group life itself—can lapse without necessarily dimming people's determination to be counted as Indians."[28]

It should not be surprising that the enemies of anti-racist activism deliberately misrepresent our strategic political, cultural, and intellectual formulations as biological essentialism. In so doing, they shift our gaze away from critiques of normativity and whiteness, putting us on the defensive as if we were the authors of the racist categories we find ourselves forced to confront. Yet some of our own underlying assumptions sometimes encourage these distortions. Too often, we take our own history for granted, and fail to foreground some of the lessons we have learned over the years through long and difficult struggle.

Like most social movements of the industrial era, the anti-racist activism of the civil rights era relied on the solidarity of sameness. We built organic solidarity around common experiences and common identities, deciding that those identities (like race) gave us commonalities that were more important than our differences. We knew that all ethnic groups are coalitions, that all identities are socially constructed, that there was never one way to be Black, or one way to be a worker, or one way to be a citizen, or one way to be gay or lesbian. But especially given the pressures on us to dis-identify with low status groups, it was often extremely satisfying to be with people who seemed similar to ourselves, people with the same language, religion, skin color, cuisine, or culture. Radical solidarity based on a common racial identity not only turned negative ascription into positive affirmation, it also functioned as an alternative to the radical divisiveness and dis-identification that often plagues aggrieved groups because their members are constantly in competition with one another for scarce resources and limited prestige, who see a mirror of their own humiliation and debasement in the faces of people who look just like them.

Yet this organic solidarity often exacted a high price by making us expect to find (or feign) more uniformity within groups than actually existed. It encouraged us to seek uniformity rather than unity, to confuse identicality with identity. By denying the divisions that existed within our own ranks, we deprived ourselves of the dynamism of difference—the consciousness and knowledge that can only come from seeing a problem from more than one perspective, the processes that fashion group identity from the full range, complexity, and contradictions of collective experience. Moreover, the desire for sameness always leads to disappointment, to divisive fights about who is Chicano enough or Black enough or Indian enough. As Maryse Conde argues in respect to the legacy of *negritude* in the francophone Caribbean, the exhilarating promises of "likeness" and "similarity" that nationalist mobilizations promoted only set the stage for deep disillusionment and sectarian divisiveness when Afro-Caribbeans started to realize that they could not solve their own problems through references to an idealized and undifferentiated pan-Africanism. "Without Negritude," she contends, "we would not have experienced the degree of disillusionment that we did."[29] Conde claims that emphasis on a shared pan-African identity during anti-colonial struggles often occluded gender differences, reminding us that unveiled Algerian women carried and detonated bombs in the war for independence from France, only to find themselves veiled and disenfranchised in the nation their sacrifices helped to create.

Thus, when mixed race people see themselves as lacking secure and fixed points of reference, as vexed by choices about what their identities mean, they are not different from "raced" people, people who have learned that solidarity based on identity is limited, but that solidarities based on identities are unlimited, that we cannot draw our politics from our identities, but instead must construct our identities through our politics. Racial identifications and identities are historical, socially constructed, and strategic. They are not good sources of safety, security, or certainty. They are based on legacies of belief as well as of blood and bone. Their noises and echoes come to us by choice as well as by chance; they are inherited *and* invented, found *and* fabricated, determined *and* dynamic.

Ethnic studies activists, intellectuals, and artists have often made their greatest contributions in spaces that might not seem to belong to them by birth. Chinese American ancestry does not diminish Grace Lee Boggs's contributions to the African American freedom struggle.[30] Yemeni farm worker Nagi Daifallah became a martyr to the Chicano movement when he was shot and killed by a county sheriff in California in 1973 because of his activism in the United Farm Workers union.[31] Headed by Cesar Chavez and Delores Huerta, the UFW itself emerged out of the Filipino Agricultural Workers Organizing Committee led by Larry Itliong and Philip Vera Cruz.[32] Chicano Ralph Lazo presented himself as a Japanese American during World War II and endured internment at the Manzanar Relocation Center so that he could stay with his Japanese American friends from Los Angeles's Belmont High School. "Who can say I haven't got Japanese blood in me?" Lazo asked incredulous relocation officials when they discovered his identity and ordered him released from the camp.[33] Yuri Kochiyama's internment camp experiences motivated her later participation in Malcolm X's Organization of African American Unity as well as in the Puerto Rican independence movement.[34] The flag flown by activists from AIM at Wounded Knee, South Dakota, in 1973 featured four colors— red, yellow, black, and white—to represent four races and four directions.

Although rarely acknowledged by their identities, mixed race people have routinely played important roles in progressive politics and inter-ethnic anti-racist activism. In many cases their mixed race heritage proved to be an advantage—not because of biology, but because it armed them with the situated knowledge of more than one group. William Apess's *A Eulogy on King Phillip* is one of the most powerful condemnations of North American anti-Indian racism. Its author, a participant in the Mashpee revolt, was a Christian convert who claimed a Euro-Indian father and a Pequot mother (although some scholars believe she might have been an African American slave).[35] Lucy Parsons is often celebrated for her work as a labor activist, anarchist, and communist, but rarely recognized as an individual with Mexican, Black, and Native American ancestry.[36] Bob Marley has become a global symbol of Black Nationalism, even though his father was white, and the reggae music that he is famous for emerged from the combined efforts of Black, Chinese, and East Indian artists and producers. Even the word Marley used for the Rastafarian sacramental herb, "Ganja," is of East Indian origin.[37]

The ability of raced and mixed race activists, artists, and intellectuals to draw on bloodlines of belief and to act in arenas not determined by their skin color or phenotype may hold the key to formulating a politics of mixed race identity in the present. In California today, the number of babies designated by their parents as "interracial" exceeds the number of babies designated Black, Asian American, or Native American.[38] What are the noises and the echoes that will resonate for them? What role will they play in identifying the things that divide us and the things that might unite us in the future? Will they campaign to build a panethnic collectivity out of "mixed race" identity? Will they seek to maximize their own self-interest by strategically dis-identifying with aggrieved communities of color, by seeking inclusion for themselves by policing the exclusion of others? Or will they use the particular and specific situated knowledges they possess to serve as weapons against racist exploitation and hierarchy? These choices are not so different from those confronting people who identify themselves as white, Black, Asian American, Native American, or Latino. None of us had the luxury of picking our parents or our pigment, but all of us have the obligation to pick our politics and our principles.

Social movement strategies by aggrieved racialized groups often deploy a common identity as a strategic source of organic solidarity. Yet, no single social group is ever so powerful or so united that it can secure meaningful victories on its own without any outside help. Activists in anti-racist struggles always need to change others and themselves, to bring into being new identities, identifications, and affiliations. Cultural and political activism must enact what it envisions, must produce new social relations in the course of struggle in order to bring about what Karl Marx called the alteration of people on a mass scale, ridding themselves of "the muck of ages"—the inherited and largely uninterrogated categories, classifications, characteristics, and qualities that constrain our actions and our imaginations.[39]

Strategic anti-essentialism and *branching out* have been particularly effective ways for anti-racist activists to effect affiliations and alliances grounded in inter-ethnic ideologies, epistemologies, and ontologies. Gayatri Spivak defines strategic essentialism as the tactical embrace of a single social identity in order to advance collective claims for social justice. Under conditions when the things that unite members of a particular group are more compelling than the things that divide them, strategic essentialism makes sense. When racial profiling causes police officers to stop African Americans for "driving while Black," a unified response from the Black community is warranted, regardless of that community's heterogeneity and diversity. When pervasive domestic violence threatens the safety, security, and dignity of all women, however, Black women may well want to speak out as "women," a strategic essentialism that for the moment emphasizes gender commonalities, even across racial lines.[40]

Strategic anti-essentialism, on the other hand, entails identifying with a group to which you do not belong, presenting yourself as someone else in order to express more effectively who you actually are. Willa Cather's studies of the "Orient" opened up to her a world of sensuality that she projected onto frontier life in Nebraska and New Mexico in her historical novels. Her decision to tell the story of *My Antonia* in the voice of a male narrator enabled her to express lesbian desire at a time when it would not have been possible to voice that desire directly in print.[41] Working class Blacks in New Orleans parade in the streets masquerading as Plains Indians every Mardi Gras day and every St. Joseph's day because playing "Indian" enables them to take on the identity of heroic warriors resisting white oppression without bringing on direct repression from the local white power structure. Yet the message came through clearly to other Blacks. Community activist Jerome Smith remembers thinking of Mardi Gras Indians as part of a culture that "unconsciously made statements about black power... the whole thing about excellence, about uniqueness, about creativity, about protecting your creativity."[42]

Strategic anti-essentialism can enable open expression of suppressed parts of one's own identity. Yet in depending upon racial disguise, it can do more to harm than to help anti-racist efforts. Inhabitants of the actual "Orient" were not aided by Willa Cather's appropriation of Orientalist stereotypes, and the cause of American Indians could hardly be helped by the Mardi Gras Indians' reiteration of Indian stereotypes from Wild West shows, dime novels, and John Ford films. When coupled with "branching out," however, strategic anti-essentialism can serve broader purposes.

Juan Flores identifies "branching out" as a characteristic cultural and political strategy of Puerto Ricans in New York. Defamed and discriminated against as foreigners even though they are U.S. citizens, relegated to low-wage jobs and restricted to crowded barrios while enduring ridicule for failing to "assimilate," and rejected as a racial menace to North American whiteness even though they did not think of themselves as "nonwhite" in Puerto Rico, Nuyoricans fashion a selective connection to and interaction with North American cultures, "branching out" to Black Americans, other migrants from Latin America and the Caribbean, other "unwanted" groups like Chinese Americans and Arab Americans, and "more cautiously" to Irish, Italian, and Jewish Americans, without ever seeking absorption (and deracination) in a "white" center. The polylateral points of connection afforded by "branching out" enable Puerto Rican New Yorkers opportunities to remain "ethnic" without being either "always ethnic" or "only ethnic," to create new identities without having to surrender the historical consciousness and situated knowledges specific to their group.[43]

The odyssey of musician Lee Brown offers an illustrative demonstration of the utility of strategic anti-essentialism and branching out. Born into an African American family in Newark, New Jersey in 1919, Brown remembers his youth as a constant battle against segregation and discrimination. In an autobiography published in 1967, he presents himself as someone who lived by the precepts of the Black Power movement all his life. He claims that when he was twenty years old he was so angered by the practices of motion picture theatre managers in Newark that restricted African Americans to seats only in the balcony, that he joined a delegation attempting to negotiate a change in policy. When their overtures were rejected, they resorted to direct action. "One Sunday when the theatre was filled to capacity," he recalls, "we all got up in different parts of the balcony and shouted FIRE!! We repeated this procedure every week for a month and colored people began to sit in orchestra seats."[44] Brown presents incident after incident where he and his friends break the color line through some form of militant direct action.

Yet the "essentialist" Black Power strategies popular in the 1960s when Brown wrote his book do not always conform to the strategies he reports himself pursuing in actual engagements with racialized power. These draw more on strategic anti-essentialism and on branching out than on Black nationalism. Brown learned early that racial ambiguity could work in his favor. When the musicians' union refused to admit him and his band members into the all white Local, light-skinned Pancho Diggs joined on his own because he was able to pass for white. Union officials were furious when they discovered they had admitted a Black member, but because Diggs had a valid union card, they could not prevent the whole band from receiving union scale. Once the dual wage system was broken, the union relented and allowed Brown and the other musicians to join.[45]

Brown chafed at the restrictions imposed on him as a young Black man in Newark. He found himself barred from employment by the city's largest and best paying companies, and he had to watch high school classmates with grades far worse than his secure jobs for which he was turned down. He wanted a better job than the ones that seemed available to him, so he hit upon a novel strategy. He noted the popularity of "Sabu, the Elephant Boy," a South Asian character then popular in B motion pictures, and noticed that Sabu's skin color was similar to his own. Brown approached a seamstress and commissioned her to make him some turbans. His friends just laughed when they saw him dressed as Sabu, but Brown discovered that white people who did not know him showed him much more respect in a turban than they had when they believed him to have been an American Black.[46]

Brown began calling himself "Ram Singh," moved to Los Angeles, and secured a job as chauffeur to Hollywood film star Errol Flynn. He found that Ram Singh could do things that Lee Brown could not: stay in luxury hotels, date white women, and draw respectful bows "from the southern ofays" in his neighborhood.[47] Brown carried his disguise to a new level after working for Flynn for eight months. The actor was accused of having sex with underage girls and did not want his chauffeur available for questioning by the police, so he paid Ram Singh $500 to leave town. But before he could depart, Brown experienced a sudden appendicitis attack and had to be taken to a hospital emergency room. The cab driver who drove him there noticed that he had passed out, and stole his wallet before dumping him at the hospital. None of the physicians knew who he was and Brown had no proof of his identity. Not wishing to be Lee Brown again, but unable to continue as Ram Singh to protect Errol Flynn, Brown told his doctors that his name was Babs Gonzales. Brown claims that as a child, he and each of his three brothers were nicknamed Babs, which if true, must have presented some difficulties for people trying to reach them by phone. The "Gonzales" was a generic Spanish surname that Brown chose because he believed he would encounter less discrimination as a Mexican American than he would as an African American.

Brown bought a Spanish language dictionary and started associating with Mexican street hustlers on Sixth Street in downtown Los Angeles. His local draft board in Newark was looking for Lee Brown, but since he secured legal papers as Babs Gonzales, he wasn't worried. But his mother told federal officers where he was, and then followed him to Los Angeles and sent him back east by bus. On the journey, he spoke only Spanish so that he could be served at bus station lunch counters, even bringing back food for two Black women on the bus whose patronage was unwelcome at the very lunch counters who provided service to Babs Gonzales, a "Mexican."

An additional disguise was necessary before he could escape the draft. The man known as Lee Brown, Ram Singh, and Babs Gonzales reported to his pre-induction physical in Newark wearing women's clothes and with his toenails and fingernails painted bright red. When the army rejected him, he was free to become Babs Gonzales again, and resume his career as a jazz pianist and singer. He enjoyed great success putting lyrics to bebop instrumentals, and as the leader of Three Bips and a Bop, he enjoyed international recognition and acclaim. A stint in Paris enabled him to learn enough French to cross the color line in a restaurant in Atlanta, Georgia. When no one offered him service, Gonzales began speaking loudly in French, and fearing an international incident, the manager not only served him, but picked up the tab for his drinks.[48]

It is not completely clear whether the autobiography of Lee Brown/Ram Singh/Babs Gonzales is an accurate account of events or simply another exercise in creative masquerade. His punctuation puts everyone's name in quotation marks, as if "Ben Webster," "James Moody," and "Harry Edison" might be pseudonyms. He even puts the names of cities in quotation marks, as if "Newark," "Paterson," and "Trenton" might really be named Lee Brown, Ram Singh, or Babs Gonzales. But even if it is only performance, the book is a powerful example of how strategic anti-essentialism and branching out can augment opportunities and allow for the elasticity of identities.[49] Brown's story is similar to that of Johnny Otis—an ethnic Greek who became "Black by persuasion"—to Little Julian Herrera—the first Chicano doo wop rock'n'roll heart throb who was really a Hungarian Jew—to Korla Pandit—an African American from Missouri who for nearly fifty years fooled television viewers and exotica music fans into thinking he was a high caste Brahmin from India—to Narcisso Martinez who sold recordings of polkas under his own name to Mexicans, but marketed the same recordings as "Louisiana Pete" when selling to Cajuns and "the Polski Kwartet" when selling to Polish Americans. Lee Brown combated the everyday indignities of racial discrimination by carrying social construction to an extreme. By proving that identities can be learned and performed, strategic anti-essentialism and branching out can sometimes show that belief and belonging is not always a matter of blood or bone.

Asian Immigrant Women Advocates originated as an Asian American feminist organization committed to advancing the interests of new Asian immigrant women. But they found that job segmentation and environmental racism mandated that any efforts to help Asian immigrant women had to assist Latinas as well. Korean Immigrant Worker Advocates in Los Angeles started out trying to organize Korean low wage workers in Los Angeles sweatshops and restaurants. They discovered that in order to help Korean low wage workers, they had to ally with Latino/a workers against Korean immigrant capitalists. The Bus Riders Union in Los Angeles formed to challenge the neighborhood race effects that leave inner city bus riders with expensive but inefficient transportation as a way of subsidizing luxury trains for suburban commuters. Their multi-racial organizing team realized that transit racism meant that the fifteen percent of inner city bus riders who are white suffer from neighborhood race effects aimed at people of color, and that the small percentage of suburban train riders who are people of color benefit from the possessive investment in whiteness. Consequently, they filed a civil rights suit to challenge transit racism. The suit stipulated that for purposes of this case, that the inner city bus riders who are white should be treated as people of color and that the suburban train riders who are African American, Native American, or Asian American should be treated as if they were white. The Bus Riders Union won a settlement because of that suit, a settlement that has brought lower fares and better service to inner city bus riders on new non-polluting buses purchased solely because of the Bus Riders Union's activism.

The pain and political frustrations of mixed race people are real. They cannot be wished away by glib formulations or erased by the example of a few inspired eccentrics. Like all racial identities, the "mixed race" category can neither be entirely embraced nor entirely evaded. But it can be analyzed, and understood, and utilized as a standpoint from which to fight against all forms of dehumanization, exploitation, oppression, and suppression, following the example of race-specific activism by Asian Immigrant Women Advocates and Korean Immigrant Workers Advocates as well as by the consciously multi-ethnic organizing of the Bus Riders Union. As an embodied identity, "mixed race" is an accident of history. As an epistemology and a situated knowledge, as a standpoint from which to create strategic anti-essentialism and branching out, it is a powerful weapon of the struggle available to everyone.

In her poem "Child of the Americas," Aurora Levins Morales proclaims her identity as a "light-skinned mestiza of the Caribbean, a child of many diaspora, born into this continent at a crossroads." Levins Morales goes on to explicate her particularly complicated family history and its enduring meanings for her. Like the Yoruba elders of West Africa and the Vodou believers in Haiti, she focuses on the trope of the "crossroads"—the place where different paths converge, where painful collisions happen, but also the place where moral and political choices can make things better. Speaking literally for herself, but figuratively for all of us, she concludes

I am not African. Africa is in me, but I cannot return.
I am not Taina, Taino is in me, but there is no way back.
I am not European. Europe lives in me, but I have no home there.

I am new. History made me. My first language was spanglish.
I was born at the crossroads
And I am whole.[50]

Notes

1. Moris Moriset is president of the Haitian rara group, Rara Ti-Malis Kache. He is quoted by Elizabeth McAlister at the beginning of her very important book, *Rara! Vodou, Power, and Performance in Haiti and its Diaspora* (Berkeley: University of California Press, 2002).

2. W. E. B. Du Bois, *Black Reconstruction in America* (New York: Touchstone, 1995) 52.

3. Albert Memmi, *Racism* (Minneapolis: University of Minnesota Press, 2000), 7.

4. Pauline Tuner Strong and Barril Van Winkle, " 'Indian Blood': Reflections on the Reckoning and Reconfiguring of a Native North American Identity," *Cultural Anthropology* v.11 n.4 (November) 1996, 551.

5. Carolyn Cooper, *Noises in the Blood: Orality, Gender, and the 'Vulgar' Body of Jamaican Popular Culture* (Durham: Duke University Press, 1995), 4. Jamaican dramatist Dennis Scott's 1974 play *An Echo in the Bone* may have influenced Reid's 1983 novel. See also Joseph Roach, *Cities of the Dead: Circum Atlantic Performance* (New York: Columbia University Press, 1996).

6. Vincent Harding has warned against reducing the struggle to merely desegregating the ranks of the pain inflictors of this world. Charlotta Bass argued against settling for "dark faces in high places."

7. Timothy Beneke, "Curriculum for a New California," *Express* v.21 n.50, September 17, 1999, 10.

8. Chris Iijima, "Pontifications on the Distinction between Grains of Sand and Yellow Pearls," in Steve Louie and Glenn Omatsu, ed., *Asian Americans: The Movement and the Moment* (Los Angeles: UCLA Asian American Studies Center Press, 2001), 7.

9. Roberta Hill Whiteman (now Roberta Hill), *Philadelphia Flowers: Poems by Roberta Hill Whiteman* (Duluth, Minnesota: Holy Cow Press, 1996), 89.

10. Ibid., 91.

11. Elizabeth McAlister, *Rara! Vodou Power, and Performance in Haiti and Its Diaspora* (Berkeley: University of California Press, 2002), 49. Sterling Stuckey, *Slave Culture: Nationalist Theory and the Foundations of Black America* (New York: Oxford, 1987).

12. Helena Simonett, *Banda: Mexican Musical Life Across Borders* (Middletown, Connecticut: Wesleyan University Press, 2001), 57.

13. Rachel Buff, *Immigration and the Political Economy of Home: West Indian Brooklyn and American Indian Minneapolis, 1945–1992* (Berkeley: University of California Press, 2001), 147–70.

14. W.E.B Du Bois, *The Souls of Black Folk* (New York: Fawcett Publications, 1961), 181, 183–84.

15. Frederick Douglass, *Narrative of the Life of Frederick Douglass, An American Slave* (Middlesex: Harmondsworth, 1982), 57–58.

16. L. Frank, *Acorn Soup* (Berkeley: Heyday Books, 1999), 10.

17. Nellie Wong, "The Art and Politics of Asian American Women," in Fred Ho, ed., with Carolyn Antonio, Diane Fujino, Steve Yip, *Legacy to Liberation: Politics and Culture of Revolutionary Asian Pacific America* (San Francisco: Big Red Media, AK Press, 2000), 235.

18. Lorna Dee Cervantes, "Visions of Mexico While Attending a Writing Symposium in Port Townsend, Washington," in *Emplumada* (Pittsburgh: University of Pittsburgh Press, 1981), 45.

19. Farah Jasmine Griffin, *"Who Set You Flowin'?" The African American Migration Narrative* (New York: Oxford, 1995).

20. Quoted in M. Jacqui Alexander, "Erotic Autonomy as a Politics of Decolonization: An Anatomy of Feminist and State Practice in the Bahamas Tourist Economy," in M. Jacqui Alexander and Chandra Talpede Mohanty, *Feminist Genealogies, Colonial Legacies, Democratic Futures* (New York and London: Routledge, 1997), 63.

21. Lori Andrews, *Black Power, White Blood: The Life and Times of Johnny Spain* (Philadelphia: Temple University Press, 1999).

22. George Lipsitz, *American Studies in a Moment of Danger* (Minneapolis: University of Minnesota Press, 2001), 10–12. Figures like these are of special interest as well to neo-liberal opponents of movements for racial justice.

23. David Parker and Miri Song, "Introduction: Rethinking 'Mixed Race,'" in David Parker and Miri Song, ed., *Rethinking 'Mixed Race'* (London: Pluto Press, 2001), 1.

24. David A. Hollinger, *Postethnic America* (New York: Basic Books, 1995), 166.

25. George J. Sanchez, " 'Y tu, que?' (Y2K): Latino History in the New Millennium," in Marcelo M. Suarez-Orozco and Mariela M. Paez, ed., *Latinos: Remaking America* (Berkeley: University of California Press, 2002), 54.

26. France Winddance Twine, *Racism in a Racial Democracy: The Maintenance of White Supremacy in Brazil* (New Brunswick, New Jersey: Rutgers University Press, 1998).

27. Nicole Davis, "Racefile" *ColorLines Action* v.4 n.2 (Summer) 2001, 1.

28. Alexandra Harmon, "Wanted: More Histories of Indian Identity," in Philip J. Deloria and Neal Salisbury, eds., *A Companion to American Indian History* (Malden, Massachusetts: Blackwell, 2002), 261.

29. Maryse Conde, "Pan-Africanism, Feminism, and Culture," in Sidney Lemelle and Robin D.G. Kelley, eds., *Imagining Home: Class, Culture, and Nationalism in the African Diaspora* (London: Verso, 1994), 60.

30. Grace Lee Boggs, *Living For Change: An Autobiography* (Minneapolis: University of Minnesota Press, 1998).

31. Nabeel Abraham, "Arab Americans," in Mari Jo Buhle, Paul Buhle, and Dan Georgakus, eds., *Encyclopedia of the American Left* (New York: Oxford University Press, second edition, 1998), 58.

32. E. San Juan, "Filipinos," in Mari Jo Buhle, Paul Buhle, and Dan Georgakus, eds., *Encyclopedia of the American Left* (New York: Oxford University Press, second edition, 1998), 225.

33. Beatrice Griffith, *American Me* (Cambridge: Houghton Mifflin, 1948), 321.

34. Yuri Kochiyama, *Discover Your Mission: Selected Speeches and Writings of Yuri Kochiyama* (Los Angeles: UCLA Asian American Studies Center, 1998).

35. Richard White, "On the Beaches," *London Review of Books*, March 21, 2002, 26.

36. Gary Nash, "The Hidden History of Mestizo America," *Journal of American History* v.82 n.3 (December) 1995.

37. Timothy White, *Catch a Fire: The Life of Bob Marley* (New York: Henry Holt and Company, 1998), 15–16, 114–15.

38. Kelvin M. Pollard and William P. O'Hare, "America's Racial and Ethnic Minorities," *Population Bulletin* v.54 n.3 (1999), 13.

39. Karl Marx, "The German Ideology," in Robert C. Tucker, ed., *The Marx-Engels Reader* (New York and London: W.W. Norton and Company, 1978), 193.

40. Gayatri Spivak, *Outside in the Teaching Machine* (New York and London: Routledge, 1993), 3–4. Spivak's argument prefigured Lisa

Lowe's deployment of multiplicity. See Lisa Lowe, "Heterogeneity, Hybridity, and Multiplicity: Marking Asian American Differences," *Diaspora* v.1 n.1 (1991), 28.

41. Sharon O'Brien, *Willa Cather: The Emerging Voice* (New York: Oxford, 1987), 136–37, 205–06.

42. Kim Lacy Rodgers, *Righteous Lives* (New York: New York University Press, 1993), 111–12.

43. Juan Flores, " 'Que Assimilated, Brother, Yo Soy Assimilao': The Structuring of Puerto Rican Identity in the U.S.," *Journal of Ethnic Studies* v.13 n.3, n.d., 1–16 .

44. Babs Gonzales, *I Paid My Dues, Good Times... No Bread, A Story of Jazz* (East Orange, New Jersey: Expubidence Publishing, 1967), 14.

45. Ibid., 14–15.

46. Confounding U.S. national racial categories by referring to acceptance of non-white foreigners in places U.S. Blacks could not go is an old trope. Booker T. Washington uses it in *Up From Slavery*. Malcolm X used it as well.

47. Ibid., 20–21. Sabu starred in *The Elephant Boy* (1937) and went on to star in movies connected to the jungle: *Drums* (1938), *Jungle Book* (1942), and *Jungle Hell* (1955), and in a dose of interchangeable orientalism *The Thief of Baghdad* (1940) and *Arabian Nights* (1942). Vijay Prashad, *The Karma of Brown Folk* (Minneapolis: University of Minnesota Press, 2000), 28.

48. Ibid., 138.

49. Donald Clarke, ed., *The Penguin Encyclopedia of Popular Music* (London: Penguin, 1990), 473. Babs Gonzales, *I Paid My Dues, Good Times... No Bread, A Story of Jazz* (East Orange, New Jersey: Expubidence Publishing), 1967.

50. Aurora Levins Morales, "Child of the Americas," in *Boricuas: Influential Puerto Rican Writings—An Anthology*, Roberto Santiago, ed., (New York: One World, 1995), 79.

Bibliography

Abraham, Nabeel "Arab Americans," in Mari Jo Buhle, Paul Buhle, and Dan Georgakus, ed., *Encyclopedia of the American Left* (New York: Oxford University Press, second edition, 1998)

Alexander, M. Jacqui "Erotic Autonomy as a Politics of Decolonialization: An Anatomy of Feminist and State Practice in the Bahamas Tourist Economy," in M. Jacqui Alexander and Chandra Mohanty, eds., *Feminist Genealogies, Colonial Legacies, Democratic Futures* (New York and London: Routledge, 1997)

Andrews, Lori *Black Power, White Blood: The Life and Times of Johnny Spain* (Philadelphia: Temple University Press, 1999)

Beneke, Timothy "Curriculum for a New California," *Express* v.21 n.50 September 17, 1999, 10

Boggs, Grace Lee *Living for Change: An Autobiography* (Minneapolis: University of Minnesota Press, 1998)

Buff, Rachel *Immigration and the Political Economy of Home: West Indian Brooklyn and American Indian Minneapolis, 1945–1992* (Berkeley: University of California Press, 2001)

Cervantes, Lorna Dee "Visions of Mexico While Attending A Writing Symposium in Port Townsend, Washington," in *Emplumada* (Pittsburgh: University of Pittsburgh Press, 1981)

Clarke, Donald, ed., *The Penguin Encyclopedia of Popular Music* (London: Penguin, 1990)

Conde, Maryse, "Pan-Africanism, Feminism, and Culture," in Sidney Lemelle and Robin D.G. Kelley, ed., *Imagining Home: Class, Culture, and Nationalism in the African Diaspora* (London: Verso, 1994)

Cooper, Carolyn *Noises in the Blood: Orality, Gender, and the 'Vulgar' Body of Jamaican Popular Culture* (Durham: Duke University Press, 1995)

Davis, Nicole "Racefile," *Color Lines Action* v.4 n.2 (Summer) 2001

Du Bois, W.E.B. *Black Reconstruction in America* (New York: Touchstone, 1995)

Du Bois, W.E.B. *The Souls of Black Folk* (New York: Fawcett Publications, 1961)

Douglass, Frederick *Narrative of the Life of Frederick Douglass, An American Slave* (Middlesex: Harmondsworth, 1982)

Flores, Juan "Que Assimilated Brother, *Yo Soy Assimilao*': The Structuring of Puerto Rican Identity in the U.S.," *Journal of Ethnic Studies* v.13 n.3 n.d.

Frank, L., *Acorn Soup* (Berkeley: Heyday Books, 1999)

Gonzales, Babs *I Paid My Dues, Good Times ... No Bread, A Story of Jazz* (East Orange, New Jersey: Expubidence Publishing, 1967)

Griffin, Farah Jasmine *Who Set You Flowin'? The African American Migration Narrative* (New York: Oxford, 1995)

Griffith, Beatrice *American Me* (Cambridge: Houghton Mifflin, 1948)

Harmon, Alexandra "Wanted: More Histories of Indian Identity," in Philip J. Deloria and Neal Salisbury, ed., *A Companion to American Indian History* (Malden, MA: Blackwell, 2002)

Hollinger, David A. *Postethnic America* (New York: Basic Books, 1995)

Iijima, Chris "Pontifications on the Distinction Between Grains of Sand and Yellow Pearls," in Steve Louie and Glenn Omatsu, ed., *Asian Americans: The Movement and the Moment* (Los Angeles: UCLA Asian American Studies Center Press, 2001)

Kochiyama, Yuri *Discover Your Mission: Selected Speeches and Writings of Yuri Kochiyama* (Los Angeles: UCLA Asian American Studies Center, 1998)

Lipsitz, George *American Studies in a Moment of Danger* (Minneapolis: University of Minnesota, 2001)

Lowe, Lisa "Heterogeneity, Hybridity, and Multiplicity: Marking Asian American Differences," *Diaspora* v.1 n.1 (1991)

Marx, Karl "The German Ideology," in Robert C. Tucker, ed. *The Marx-Engels Reader* (New York and London: W.W. Norton and Company, 1978)

McAlister, Elizabeth *Rara! Vodou, Power, and Performance in Haiti and Its Diaspora* (Berkeley: University of California Press, 2002)

Memmi, Albert *Racism* (Minneapolis: University of Minnesota Press, 2000)

Morales, Aurora Levins "Child of the Americas," in Robert Santiago, ed., *Boricuas: Influential Puerto Rican Writings—an Anthology* (New York: One World, 1995)

Nash, Gary "The Hidden History of Mestizo America," *Journal of American History* v.82 n.3 (December) 1995

O'Brien, Sharon *Willa Cather: The Emerging Voice* (New York: Oxford, 1987)

Parker, David and Miri Song, "Introduction: Rethinking Mixed Race," in David Parker and Miri Song, ed., *Rethinking 'Mixed Race'* (London: Pluto Press, 2001)

Pollard, Kelvin M. and William P. O'Hare, "America's Racial and Ethnic Minorities," *Population Bulletin* v.54 n.3 (1999)

Prashad, Vijay *The Karma of Brown Folk* (Minneapolis: University of Minnesota Press, 2000)

Rogers, Kim Lacy *Righteous Lives* (New York: New York University Press, 1993)

San Juan, E. "Filipinos," in Mari Jo Buhle, Paul Buhle, and Dan Georgakus, ed., *Encyclopedia of the American Left* (New York: Oxford University press, second edition, 1998)

Sanchez, George J " '*Y tu qu*' (Y2K): Latino History in the New Millennium," in Marcelo M. Suarez-Orozco and Mariela M. Paez, ed., *Latinos: Remaking America* (Berkeley: University of California Press, 2002)

Simonett, Helena *Banda: Mexican Musical Life Across Borders* (Middletown, Connecticut: Wesleyan University Press, 2001)

Spivak, Gayatri *Outside in the Teaching Machine* (New York and London: Routledge, 1993)

Strong, Pauline Turner, and Barril Van Winkle, "'Indian Blood: Reflections on the Reckoning and Reconfiguring of a Native North American Identity," *Cultural Anthropology* v.11 n.4 (November) 1996

Stuckey, Sterling *Slave Culture: Nationalist Theory and the Foundations of Black America* (New York: Oxford, 1987)

Twine, France Winddance *Racism in a Racial Democracy: The Maintenance of White Supremacy in Brazil* (New Brunswick, New Jersey: Rutgers University Press, 1998)

White, Richard "On the Beaches," *London Review of Books*, March 21, 2002

White, Timothy *Catch A Fire: The Life of Bob Marley* (New York: Henry Holt and Company, 1998)

Whiteman, Roberta Hill *Philadelphia Flowers: Poems by Roberta Hill Whiteman* (Duluth, Minnesota: Holy Cow Press, 1996)

Wong, Nellie "The Art and Politics of Asian American Women," in Fred Ho, ed., with Carolyn Antonio, Diane Fujino, Steve Yip, *Legacy to Liberation: Politics and Culture of Revolutionary Asian Pacific America* (San Francisco: Big Red Media, AK Press, 2000)

Does Multiraciality Lighten? Me-Too Ethnicity and the Whiteness Trap

PAUL SPICKARD

University of California, Santa Barbara

Multiraciality Studies and Whiteness Studies

The two most striking themes—some would say movements—in recent ethnic studies literature are expressions of multiraciality and studies of Whiteness.[1] There are similarities and perhaps connections between there two themes. Both depend on an understanding that race is a constructed entity rather than a biological essence. Both Whiteness studies and mutiracialism have been put forth by their advocates as expressions of anti-racism. And both have been accused by their detractors of selling out the interests of people of color. It is true that there are potential dangers for monoracial communities of color in both the Whiteness studies movement and the multiracial movement. It is also true that the multiracial movement has been more concerned with the psychological needs of individuals than with the needs of monoracial communities. But, as we shall see, the dangers are greater in Whiteness studies than in the multiracial idea. Critics' fears to the contrary, the acknowledgement of multiraciality, even the assertion of a multiracial identity, is not necessarily an indicator that one is abandoning one's community of color and seeking after Whiteness.

This article to appear in *New Faces in a Changing America: Multiracial Identity in the 21st Century,* eds. Loretta I. Winters and Herman L. DeBose, Sage Publications, Thousand Oaks, California.

The concept of multiraciality needs no introduction to many readers. It is true, for good or for ill, that the last decade and a half of the twentieth century saw the rise of a new consciousness of racial multiplicity, both on the part of people who were claiming multiracial identities and in the minds of monoracial observers. In recent years the shelf of books on multiraciality has been growing rapidly (e.g., Davis 1991, Khanga 1992, Root 1992, Forbes 1993, Tizard and Phoenix 1993, Zack 1993, Camper 1994, Funderburg 1994, Haizlip 1994, Leslie 1995, Nunez 1995, Obama 1995, Scales-Trent 1995, Talalay 1995, West 1995, Williams 1995, Zack 1995, Lazarre 1996, McBride 1996, Minerbrook 1996, Root 1996a, Azoulay 1997, Eaton 1997, Hall 1997, Katz 1997, Penn 1997, Sollors 1997, J. M. Spencer 1997, O'Hearn 1998, Senna 1998a, Ball 1999, Gaskins 1999, Hara and Keller 1999, Korgen 1999, McKelvey 1999, R. Spencer 1999, Kim 2000, Spickard and Burroughs 2000, Hügel-Marshall 2001, Parker and Song 2001, Williams-León and Nakashima 2001, Daniel 2002, and of course the present volume). Ethnic studies departments have begun to recognize this trend. Courses on multiraciality are taught at several universities across the country.[2] Courses and textbooks on race and ethnicity routinely now include units on multiraciality (e.g., Thompson and Tyagi 1996, Cornell and Hartmann 1997). In 1999 San Francisco State University's College of Ethnic Studies advertised for and hired a professor whose task was specifically to teach multiracial issues.

Alongside the heightened attention to multiraciality, the 1990s witnessed a boom in Whiteness studies. Scholars began to examine the experiences of European Americans as a racial group. The impetus came from left-wing White scholars who wanted to examine the bases and processes of White privilege so that they might undermine it. The list of books in this field is just as long as that in multiraciality studies (e.g., Saxton 1990, Roediger 1991, Frankenberg 1993, Allen 1994, Almaguer 1994, Morrison 1994, Reddy 1994, Roediger 1994, Ignatiev 1995, Haney López 1996, Ignatiev and Garvey 1996, Lazarre 1996, Transition 1996, Allen 1997, Delgado and Stefancic 1997, Dyer 1997, Fine 1997, Foley 1997, Frankenberg 1997, Hill 1997, Wray and Newitz 1997, Babb 1998, Brodkin 1998, Deloria 1998, Ferber 1998, Gabriel 1998, Goad 1998, Hale 1998, Jacobson

1998, Kincheloe 1998, Lipsitz 1998, Nelson 1998, Roediger 1998, Berger 1999, Clark and O'Donnell 1999, Cuomo and Hill 1999, Hartigan 1999, Lee 1999, Nakayama and Martin 1999, Thandeka 1999, Crooks 2000, Curry 2000, Rodriguez and Villaverde 2000, Bronwen 2001, Conley 2001). The American Historical Association and the American Studies Association have held sessions on the history and culture of Whiteness. Can the establishment of faculty positions in Whiteness studies be far behind?[3]

Racial Constructions

The notion of multiraciality and the advocacy of Whiteness studies each depends on a constructivist concept of ethnicity. In a book on multiracial identity, I have argued (Spickard, 1992):

> The process of racial labeling starts with geography, culture, and family ties and runs through economics and politics to biology, and not the other way around. That is, a group is defined by an observer according to its location, its cultural practices, or its social connectedness (and their subsequent economic, social, and political implications). Then, on looking at physical markers or genetic makeup, the observer may find that this group shares certain items with greater frequency than do other populations that are also socially defined.... All of this is not to argue that there is no biological aspect to race, only that biology is not fundamental. The origins of race are sociocultural and political, and the main ways race is used are sociocultural and political. (p. 16)

In *The Sweeter the Juice* (1994), one of several books on a similar theme, Shirlee Taylor Haizlip shows half of her racially mixed family creating themselves as Black people, the other half creating themselves as White. In "A Bill of Rights for Racially Mixed People," Maria Root (1996b) argues passionately that people of mixed ancestry ought not be bound by someone else's notions of racial categories or appropriate racial behavior. She argues that, as a multiracial person:

> I have the right ...
> not to keep the races separate within me
> not to be responsible for people's discomfort with my
>   physical ambiguity
> not to justify my ethnic legitimacy

I have the right
>to identify myself differently than strangers expect
>>me to identify
>to identify myself differently than how my parents
>>identify me
>to identify myself differently than my brothers and
>>sisters
>to identify myself differently in different situations. (p. 7)

This is a powerful statement about race as individual choice, as something plastic that may—and perhaps must—be molded by individuals on a daily basis.

In an equally constructivist vein, Matthew Jacobson (1998) writes of Whiteness as "alchemy." He portrays the White group in American history as a coalition with ever-changing boundaries around it and constantly morphing glue holding it together. Karen Brodkin (1998) writes (though I think her argument is overstated) about "how Jews became White folks." David Roediger (1991), in a much more careful exposition with less sweeping claims, shows how White working people in the nineteenth century gathered in class solidarity, in part on the basis of an increasing sense of racial solidarity. The most boldly constructivist of all the Whiteness studies writers is Noel Ignatiev (1995). He argues that Whiteness itself is not a matter of skin color, ancestry, or anything else that might be attributed to historical or biological background. Rather, he says, Whiteness is defined by the very act of oppressing Black people.[4]

Undermining Racism

The main expressions in each literature, Whiteness and multiraciality studies, assert that they are antiracist in intent and impact. Multiracialists contend their work undermines the very categories of racism. Aubyn Fulton (1997) says, "I think the existence of [interracial individuals] is corrosive to and undermining of the current racial status quo (in this context I think that 'corrosive' and 'undermining' are good things, since I think that the current racial status quo is a bad thing and should be corroded and undermined)." Ronald Glass and Kendra Wallace (1996) insist that:

>Race cannot be ignored as a conceptual framework because
>of its theoretical inadequacy for capturing the phenomenon

of race, nor because of its simplistic use of reified notions for historically dynamic meanings and practices. Nor can the politics of race be transcended by a mental act of some sort (like a change in belief, or an act of will) nor wished away in a fantasy of color-blindness…. But an even stronger challenge to race can come from people at the margins to all racial centers; that is, from people expressive of multiracial existence and evident human variation, who resist efforts to be subdued and brought within racial orders. (p. 344)

Reginald Daniel (1992) submits that people who maintain multiracial identities are "subverting the racial divide." I have written that multiracial people by their very choice to assert a multiracial identity are "undermining the very basis of racism, its categories" (Spickard, Fong, & Ewalt, 1995).

In similar fashion, students of Whiteness say they are interrogating and thereby undermining the processes of White privilege. Some of them call their collective project "critical White studies" (Delgado & Stefancic, 1997). Noel Ignatiev and John Garvey (1996) call themselves "race traitors." And some scholars of Whiteness do in fact examine their subject in such a way as to critique White privilege. David Roediger (1991), echoing W. E. B. Du Bois, writes of "the wages of whiteness": "[T]he pleasures of whiteness could function as a 'wage' for white workers. That is, status and privileges conferred by race could be used to make up for alienating and exploitative class relationships, North and South. White workers could, and did, divine and accept their class positions by fashioning identities as 'not slaves' and as 'not Blacks'" (p. 13). George Lipsitz (1998) writes of "the possessive investment in whiteness":

> The problem with white people is not our whiteness, but our possessive investment in it. Created by politics, culture, and consciousness, our possessive investment in whiteness can be altered by those same processes, but only if we face the hard facts openly…. How can we account for the ways in which white people refuse to acknowledge their possessive investment in whiteness even as they work to increase its value every day? We can't blame the color of our skin. It must be the content of our character. (p. 233)

Critiques of Multiraciality and Whiteness Studies

Despite such aspirations to undermine racial privilege on the part of scholars and advocates of multiraciality and Whiteness studies, some critics have nonetheless derided each of these modes of study as tending to reinforce racial hierarchy and White privilege. Monoracialist critics say that advocacy of a multiracial interpretation encourages individuals to flee identification with communities of color and seek a middle social position, lightened by recognition of their ancestral multiplicity. Jon Michael Spencer (1997) accuses advocates of a multiracial identity of trying to create in America a three-tiered racial hierarchy like the one he perceives to exist in South Africa: White on top, multiracial in the middle, and Black on the bottom.[5] In a more sophisticated analysis, Rainier Spencer agrees, and goes on to argue that asserting multiraciality constitutes a racist embrace of the one-drop rule. Because nearly every person in America who has some African ancestry also has other ancestries, the only logical thing to do would be to call all African Americans multiracial people. To do so, he argues, would be to ignore the real social disabilities suffered by African Americans. He argues that good census data are needed to measure racial progress or the lack thereof, and that existing monoracial categories are the necessary categories of analysis. "The challenge for America," he says, "lies in determining how to move away from the fallacy of race while remaining aggressive in the battle against racism" (R. Spencer, 1999, p. 167).

Both of these critics—indeed, most of the criticism of the multiracial movement—has focused on the 1990s movement to change the racial categories employed by the U.S. Census. That is curious, for I read the census debate as a significant but ultimately minor issue in a much broader multiracial social movement (Spickard, 1999). Nonetheless, their opposition to both commonly espoused options, a multiracial category and multiple box checking, is echoed by some members of the public who identify themselves monoracially despite possessing multiple ancestries. Declaring his intention to eschew the chance to check more than one box on the 2000 Census and determined to check the Black box only, Michael Gelobter asks, "Should Frederick Douglass have checked white and black? Should W. E. B. Du Bois have checked white and black?" (Schemo, 2000, p. A1). For African American leaders such as Du Bois and Douglass to have acknowledged their patent multiracial ancestry, argues Gelobter, would have been for them to have abandoned common cause with other African Americans. This is the core of the monoracial argument against the expression of a multiracial identity: claiming a multiracial identity means abandoning Black America.

Critics of Whiteness studies are equally caustic. The critics complain that, whatever their antiracist intentions may be, the authors of Whiteness studies place White people at the center of attention, thus distracting from the real needs of peoples of color. Noel Ignatiev wrote a book with the title *How the Irish Became White* (1995) and Karen Brodkin followed with *How Jews Became White Folks* (1998). Soon scholars and lay people alike could be heard to remark, "You know, once [X White group] were not White, but then they became White." This amounted to a kind of me-too ethnicity. White people were saying, "Look at us. We have race, too. We are the ones who merit attention." Significant energy in ethnic studies began to shift away from examining the lives and experiences of people of color. Instead, that attention began to go to White people—who, I would contend, already were the subject of nearly the entire curriculum. Many studies of Whiteness, in this interpretation, amount to little more than me-too ethnic absorption on the part of White people.

It is that quality of self-absorption in each movement, and a related individualism, that are troubling. The central claim of the multiracial movement is that America must recognize the multiplicity in their identities as multiracial *individuals*. They tend to be opposed by the *group* claims of monoracially defined communities of color. Marie Hara and Nora Okja Keller (1999) have edited a stunning collection of poetry and prose by multiracial women. But in sixty-three sensitive evocations of the various authors' life experiences, almost no attention is paid to group needs. It is all about their own individual identity and relationship issues. Many multiracial activists are in practical fact committed to the needs of the communities of color to which they have connections, but their multiracial claim is essentially an individualistic concern. Similarly, Whiteness studies has resulted in a significant turning away from the issues of communities of color and redirecting of that scholarly energy toward White people as a group. In addition to individualism and self-concern, both intellectual movements have a trendy quality. As Danzy Senna (1998) writes, "hybridity is in"; the same can be said of Whiteness.

Connecting Multiraciality and Whiteness Studies

Whatever the merits of multiraciality and of Whiteness studies, the critics have pointed to at least potentially problematic tendencies in these two intellectual movements. It now remains to ascertain whether there is a connection between these two fields of concern. From a certain skeptical angle, one may view the assertion of a multiracial identity as a kind of Whiteness experience: centering Whiteness, de-centering monoracial oppression, and de-emphasizing the needs of communities of color. This we may call the Whiteness trap.

A UC Berkeley student, himself multiracial, complains about his classmates in Hapa Issues Forum, one of the multiracial groups on campus: "They're all Japanese-White kids from the suburbs who think that because they are part White their shit don't stink." Lisa Jones (1994) writes, "By marketing themselves as anything but black, do light-complexioned entertainers such as [Mariah] Carey become, in the eyes of most Americans, de facto whites? And do Carey and other people of color who feel more at ease representing themselves by their combination ethnic heritages, and not by race ... teach the world how to be 'raceless'? Or are they positioning themselves as a separate class along the lines of South African 'coloreds'?" (p. 201).

There may be some evidence that the assertion of a multiracial identity is related to middle-class status and experience in White contexts. Kerry Ann Rockquemore surveyed 250 college students, each of whom had one White and one Black parent. She found that those raised in middle-class White neighborhoods tended to identify themselves as biracial, whereas those raised in Black communities tended to identify themselves as monoracially Black (Rockquemore, 1998).

Jon Michael Spencer suggests that White parents with Black partners who have advocated a multiracial Census category have done so partly out of a wish for their children to avoid the disabilities of being Black in American society: "[It] is not all about the self-esteem of their mixed-race children. Some of this behavior has to do with the self-esteem of these interracially married white parents who have difficulty accepting their mixed-race children choosing black as an identity" (J. M. Spencer, 1997, p. 87). The most insistent advocate of a multiracial census option, Susan Graham of Project RACE, lends some support to such a suggestion when she says, "Nobody can tell me my children are more black than white" (Schemo, 2000, p. A1).

Conservative activist Charles Byrd, who is also a multiracialist, says, "What we need to do as a country is get rid of these stupid [racial] boxes altogether" (Schemo, 2000, p. A9). Royce Van Tassell (2000) echoes this opinion, setting forth multiraciality as a station on the way to getting rid of talking about race entirely. Van Tassel, affiliated with a right-wing action group that sponsors the Race Has No Place Project, wants to drum any consideration of race—of the causes, patterns, and consequences of racial discrimination—out of American public life. As evidence to support his claim that Americans do not want to think about race, talk about race, or collect data about the status of America's various racial communities, he cites a survey his group sponsored that claims that a large majority of Americans would describe a person of a Black parent and a White parent as multiracial. He skips several logical steps to the conclusion that "Americans want to reclaim their racial privacy, and they are tired of the government's intrusive race questions" (p. 5).

There are considerable grounds, then, to make the argument that multiraciality lightens. At the very least, the multiracial idea can give support to the position that the most important thing is an individual's self-identity. As in the cases of Van Tassel and Byrd, the concept of multiraciality may be used by people with malign motives to attack communities of color.

Does Multiraciality Lighten? Evidence From History

One may grant that there may be some measure of evidence for Rainier Spencer's fears. Some people who are not persons of good will—who do not support the interests of communities of color in the United States, and who do not want White Americans to have to take race seriously—may welcome the multiracial movement. They may try to turn it to their ends, as a way-station on the path to ignoring race (and therefore their own guilt) entirely. Yet does that mean that the critics' contention is true? Does multiraciality necessarily lighten? Contrary to the contentions of Spencer, Gelobter, and others, there is not much historical evidence that it does.

Consider the cases of several prominent Americans who acknowledged multiracial ancestry. Frederick Douglass was the most widely known African American of the nineteenth century. He was the son of a slave woman and a White man, although his features were such that he could not easily have passed for White. There was no fiercer advocate of the rights of African Americans, yet throughout his life Douglass acknowledged his White ancestry along with the Black. He insisted on travelling in an interracial social world, and in his latter years married a White woman. Douglass acknowledged his multiraciality, even as he embraced Black America fully. Gregory Stephens writes of Douglass: "In 1886, he told an audience: '[A man painting me insisted I show] my full face, for that is Ethiopian. Take my side face, said I, for that is Caucasian. But should you try my quarter face you would find it Indian. I don't know that any race can claim me, but being identified with slaves as I am, I think I know the meaning of the inquiry.' Douglass' public persona was that of a defender of the rights of Afro-Americans. But his private identity was multiethnic" (Stephens, 1999, p. 104).

Alice Dunbar-Nelson was an African American writer of the turn of the century and wife of poet Paul Laurence Dunbar. She was Black in her writing and in her political commitments. But her social world was racially mixed, and she passed for White frequently in her private life, for instance to shop in segregated White stores or to attend the theater. Reading out from Dunbar-Nelson's life to those of several of her contemporaries and successors in African American letters, Hanna Wallinger concludes "that although racial thinking determined the public utterances and creative writing of many prominent African Americans—... Charles Chesnutt, Wallace Thurman, Langston Hughes, Hallie E. Queen, and Josephine and Senator Blanche Bruce—it did not determine their personal lives to an exclusive degree" (Wallinger, in press).

Edith Maude Eaton was another of that same generation that spanned the turn of the twentieth century. She has widely been honored as the foremother of Asian American fiction. The child of English and Chinese parents, she lived in North America, took the pen name Sui Sin Far, and wrote in humane and sympathetic tones about the plight of Chinese Americans. Nonetheless, although she has been honored for her public persona as a Chinese American, she lived her personal life as a White woman (White-Parks, 1995; Spickard & Mengel, 1997).

W. E. B. Du Bois—historian, sociologist, journalist, cofounder of the NAACP, pan-Africanist—there is no more revered figure in African American history. Indeed, a Pulitzer Prize-winning author subtitled his story "Biography of a Race" (Lewis, 1993). And Du Bois was fervently committed to his identity as an African American, to the African American people, and later to the entire African diaspora. Yet in *Dusk of Dawn*, one of several autobiographies, Du Bois goes on at great length about the various strands of his European ancestry, some of it quite recent, and the degrees of his affinity with those strands. Du Bois was light of skin and European of feature, and he could easily have passed for White had he chosen to do so. He consistently recognized his multiraciality. But that did not mitigate his embrace of Blackness or his effectiveness in serving the cause of African Americans (Du Bois, 1984).

Similar stories could be told of other important figures of African American history: Mary Church Terrell, first president of the National Association of Colored Women; Mordecai Johnson, first African American president of Howard University; Walter White, novelist and longtime executive secretary of the NAACP; Jean Toomer, herald of the Harlem Renaissance; Adam Clayton Powell, Jr., flamboyant Congressmember from Harlem in the 1950s and `60s. All these were multiracial people who acknowledged, even embraced their multiraciality, and who nonetheless were leaders in one way or another of communities of color. Even Wallace D. Fard, the mysterious figure behind the founding of the Nation of Islam, and Malcolm X, the Black Muslims' fiery leader, were multiracial men who acknowledged their multiraciality, although they were less sanguine about it than Douglass or Du Bois.

Earlier in this chapter I reported that Michael Gelobter asked, "Should Frederick Douglass have checked white and black? Should W. E. B. Du Bois have checked white and black?"

(Schemo, 2000, p. A9). I think it is possible, given the shape of those men's careers and the contents of their public utterances, that they might well have chosen to check both Black and White boxes if they had lived to the time of the 2000 Census. Both they, and all the other individuals to whose lives I have just referred, identified themselves emphatically with communities of color (Black and Chinese in these cases). Yet they all also acknowledged their multiplicity and did not try to mask it. Some, like Dunbar-Nelson and Sui Sin Far, lived part of the time on the White side of the line. Some, like Du Bois, gloried in their multiraciality even as they chose monoracial lives. Some, like Malcolm X, hated their White ancestry. But all recognized their multiplicity even as they chose to serve communities of color. There is just not adequate historical evidence to conclude that acknowledgement or embrace of a multiracial identity necessarily lightens. The important issue for monoracial communities of color is not whether multiracial people claim their multiraciality, but whether, having done so, they continue to serve the needs of those communities of color.

The criticism of the multiracial movement—that it is a form of seeking after Whiteness—has theoretical validity: it points to a real danger. There are those who advocate a multiracial identity who also would like to do away with consideration of race in American society, who in effect would abandon the needs of communities of color. However, examining the actual lives of several multiracial people in historical context suggests that recognition, even embrace, of a multiracial identity does not mean that multiracial people fall into the Whiteness trap.

Notes

1. In this chapter I capitalize such words as "White," "Black," and "Whiteness" because they are used as proper nouns and adjectives, in the same way that "African American," "Caucasian," and "European American" are proper nouns and adjectives. I have met only a handful of people who could accurately be described to be the color black, and I have never met a White person without a tinge of pink, beige, or grey. I do not capitalize "multiracial," because, in my judgment, it is not yet an accepted racial designation in American society at large, as much as some people whom I respect would like it to be. I use it here, then, as a descriptive adjective. Some of the authors whose words I quote use a different capitalization scheme. I have left their words as they wrote them.

2. In recent years they have included the University of California campuses at Berkeley, Los Angeles, and Santa Barbara; California State University campuses at Northridge, San Francisco, and San Jose; Brigham Young University—Hawai`i; the University of Hawai`i; the University of North Texas; and Brown University.

3. Some would argue that the majority of faculty positions in the humanities and social sciences are in fact already dedicated to Whiteness studies. See Spickard, in press.

4. For a more careful exposition of racial construction on the part of African Americans in the same period, see Gomez, 1998. For theoretical formulations of racial construction, see Cornell and Hartmann, 1997 and Spickard and Burroughs, 2000. For a fuller examination of the strengths and dangers of the Whiteness studies movement, see Spickard (in press).

5. Spencer sees only two races in America, Black and White. He offers essentially no evidence for his South African analogy.

References

Allen, Theodore. (1994). *The Invention of the White Race: Racial Oppression and Social Control.* London: Verso.

Allen, Theodore. (1997). *The Invention of the White Race: The Origin of Racial Oppression in Anglo-America.* London: Verso.

Almaguer, Tomás. (1994). *Racial Fault Lines: The Historical Origins of White Supremacy in California.* Berkeley: University of California Press.

Azoulay, Katya Gibel. (1997). *Black, Jewish, and Interracial.* Durham, NC: Duke University Press.

Babb, Valerie. (1998). *Whiteness Visible: The Meaning of Whiteness in American Literature and Culture.* New York: New York University Press, 1998.

Ball, Edward. (1999). *Slaves in the Family.* New York: Random House.

Berger, Maurice. (1999). *White Lies: Race and the Myths of Whiteness.* New York: Farrar, Straus and Giroux.

Brodkin, Karen. (1998). *How Jews Became White Folks and What That Says About Race in America.* New Brunswick, NJ: Rutgers University Press.

Bronwen, Walter. (2001). *Outsiders Inside: Whiteness, Place and Irish Women.* New York: Routledge.

Camper, Carol, ed. (1994). *Miscegenation Blues: Voices of Mixed Race Women.* Toronto: Sister Vision.

Clark, Christine, and James O'Donnell, eds. (1999). *Becoming and Unbecoming White: Owning and Disowning a Racial Identity.* Westport, CT: Bergin and Garvey.

Conley, Dalton. (2000). *Honky.* Berkeley: University of California Press.

Cornell, Stephen, and Douglas Hartmann. (1997). *Ethnicity and Race.* Thousand Oaks, CA: Pine Forge Press.

Crooks, Kalpana Seshari. (2000). *Desiring Whiteness: A Lacanian Analysis of Race.* New York: Routledge.

Cuomo, Chris. J., and Kim Q. Hall, eds. (1999). *Whiteness: Feminist Philosophical Reflections.* Lanham, MD: Rowman and Littlefield.

Curry, Renee R. (2000). *White Women Writing White.* New York: Greenwood.

Daniel, G. Reginald. (1992). "Passers and Pluralists: Subverting the Racial Divide." In *Racially Mixed People in America,* ed. Maria P. P. Root. Newbury Park, CA: Sage. Pp. 91–107.

Daniel, G. Reginald. (2002). *More than Black? Multiracial Identity and the New Racial Order.* Philadelphia: Temple University Press.

Davis, F. James. (1991). *Who Is Black? One Nation's Definition.* University Park: Pennsylvania State University Press.

Delgado, Richard, and Jean Stefancic, eds. (1997). *Critical White Studies.* Philadelphia: Temple University Press.

Deloria, Philip. (1998). *Playing Indian.* New Haven, CT: Yale University Press.

Du Bois, W. E. B. (1984). *Dusk of Dawn: An Essay toward an Autobiography of a Race Concept.* New Brunswick, NJ: Transaction.

Dyer, Richard. (1997). *White.* London: Routledge.

Eaton, Winnifred. (1997). *Me: A Book of Remembrance.* Jackson: University Press of Mississippi.

Ferber, Abby L. (1998). *White Man Falling: Race, Gender, and White Supremacy.* Lanham, MD: Rowman and Littlefield.

Fine, Michelle, et al., eds. (1997). *Off White: Readings on Race, Power, and Society.* New York: Routledge.

Foley, Neil. (1997). *The White Scourge: Mexicans, Blacks, and Poor Whites in Texas Cotton Culture.* Berkeley: University of California Press.

Forbes, Jack D. (1993). *Africans and Native Americans: The Language of Race and the Evolution of Red-Black Peoples.* Urbana: University of Illinois Press.

Frankenberg, Ruth. (1993). *White Women, Race Matters: The Social Construction of Whiteness.* Minneapolis: University of Minnesota Press.

Frankenberg, Ruth, ed. (1997). *Displacing Whiteness: Essays in Social and Cultural Criticism.* Durham, NC: Duke University Press.

Fulton, Aubyn. (1997). Online posting, Interracial Individuals Discussion List, May 30 [ii-list@hcs.harvard.edu]. Quoted in Spencer, *Spurious Issue.* P. 197.

Funderburg, Lise. (1994). *Black, White, Other: Biracial Americans Talk About Race and Identity.* New York: Morrow.

Gabriel, John. (1998). *Whitewash: Racialized Politics and the Media.* New York: Routledge.

Gaskins, Pearl Fuyo. (1999). *What Are You? Voices of Mixed-Race Young People.* New York: Holt.

Glass, Ronald David, and Kendra R. Wallace. (1996). "Challenging Race and Racism: A Framework for Educators." In *The Multiracial Experience,* ed. Maria P. P. Root. Thousand Oaks, CA: Sage. Pp. 341–58.

Goad, Jim. (1998). *The Redneck Manifesto: How Hillbillies, Hicks, and White Trash Became America's Scapegoats.* New York: Touchstone.

Gomez, Michael A. (1998). *Exchanging Our Country Marks: The Transformation of African Identities and the Colonial and Antebellum South.* Chapel Hill: University of North Carolina Press.

Haizlip, Shirlee Taylor. (1994). *The Sweeter the Juice: A Family Memoir in Black and White.* New York: Simon and Schuster.

Hale, Grace Elizabeth. (1998). *Making Whiteness: The Culture of Segregation in the South, 1890–1940.* New York: Vintage.

Hall, Wade. (1997). *Passing for Black: The Life and Careers of Mae Street Kidd.* Lexington: University Press of Kentucky.

Haney López, Ian F. (1996). *White By Law: The Legal Construction of Race.* New York: New York University Press.

Hara, Marie, and Nora Okja Keller, eds. (1999). *Intersecting Circles: The Voices of Hapa Women in Poetry and Prose.* Honolulu: Bamboo Ridge.

Hartigan, John. (1999). *Racial Situations: Class Predicaments of Whiteness in Detroit.* Princeton, NJ: Princeton University Press.

Hill, Mike, ed. (1997). *Whiteness: A Critical Reader.* New York: New York University Press.

Hügel-Marshall, Ika. (2001). *Invisible Woman: Growing Up Black in Germany.* New York: Continuum.

Ignatiev, Noel. (1995). *How the Irish Became White.* New York: Routledge.

Ignatiev, Noel, and John Garvey, eds. (1996). *Race Traitor.* New York: Routledge.

Jacobson, Matthew Frye. (1998). *Whiteness of a Different Color: European Immigrants and the Alchemy of Race.* Cambridge, MA: Harvard University Press.

Jones, Lisa. (1994). *Bulletproof Diva: Tales of Race, Sex, and Hair.* New York: Doubleday.

Katz, William Loren. (1997). *Black Indians.* New York: Simon and Schuster.

Khanga, Yelena. (1992). *Soul to Soul: The Story of a Black Russian American Family, 1865–1992.* New York: Norton.

Kim, Elizabeth. (2000). *Ten Thousand Sorrows.* New York: Doubleday.

Kincheloe, Joe, et al., eds. (1998). *White Reign: Deploying Whiteness in America.* New York: St. Martin's.

Korgen, Kathleen Odell. (1999). *From Black to Biracial: Transforming Racial Identity Among Americans.* Westport, CT: Praeger.

Lazarre, Jane. (1996). *Beyond the Whiteness of Whiteness: Memoir of a White Mother of Black Sons.* Durham, NC: Duke University Press.

Lee, Robert G. (1999). *Orientals: Asian Americans in Popular Culture.* Philadelphia: Temple University Press.

Leslie, Kent Anderson. (1995). *Woman of Color, Daughter of Privilege: Amanda America Dickson, 1849–1893.* Athens: University of Georgia Press.

Lewis, David Levering. (1993). *W. E. B. Du Bois: Biography of a Race.* New York: Holt.

Lipsitz, George. (1998). *The Possessive Investment in Whiteness: How White People Profit from Identity Politics.* Philadelphia: Temple University Press.

McBride, James. (1996). *The Color of Water: A Black Man's Tribute to His White Mother.* New York: Riverhead.

McKelvey, Robert S. (1999). *The Dust of Life: America's Children Abandoned in Vietnam.* Seattle: University of Washington Press.

Minerbrook, Scott. (1996). *Divided to the Vein: A Journey into Race and Family.* New York: Harcourt Brace.

Nakayama, Thomas K., and Judith N. Martin, eds. (1999). *Whiteness: The Communication of Social Identity.* Thousand Oaks, CA: Sage.

Nunez, Sigrid. (1995). *A Feather on the Breath of God.* New York: Harper Collins.

Obama, Barack. (1995). *Dreams from My Father: A Story of Race and Inheritance.* New York: Times Books.

O'Hearn, Claudine Chiawei, ed. (1998). *Half + Half: Writers on Growing Up Biracial + Bicultural.* New York: Pantheon.

Parker, David, and Miri Song, eds. (2001). *Rethinking 'Mixed Race.'* London: Pluto.

Penn, William S., ed. (1997). *As We Are Now: Mixblood Essays on Race and Identity.* Berkeley: University of California Press.

Reddy, Maureen. (1994). *Crossing the Color Line: Race, Parenting, and Culture.* New Brunswick, NJ: Rutgers University Press.

Rockquemore, Kerry Ann. (1998). "Between Black and White: Exploring the Biracial Experience." *Race and Society.* 1.2. Pp. 197–212.

Rodriguez, Nelson M., and Leila E. Villaverde, eds. (2000). *Dismantling White Privilege: Pedagogy, Politics, and Whiteness.* New York: Peter Lang.

Roediger, David. (1991). *The Wages of Whiteness: Race and the Making of the American Working Class.* London: Verso.

Roediger, David. (1994). *Towards the Abolition of Whiteness.* London: Verso.

Root, Maria P. P., ed. (1992). *Racially Mixed People in America.* Newbury Park, CA: Sage.

Root, Maria P. P., ed. (1996a). *The Multiracial Experience.* Thousand Oaks, CA: Sage.

Root, Maria P. P. (1996b). "A Bill of Rights for Racially Mixed People." In *The Multiracial Experience,* ed. Root. Thousand Oaks, CA: Sage. Pp. 3–14.

Saxton, Alexander. (1990). *The Rise and Fall of the White Republic: Class Politics and Mass Culture in Nineteenth-Century America.* London: Verso.

Scales-Trent, Judy. (1995). *Notes of a White Black Woman.* University Park: Pennsylvania State University Press.

Schemo, Diana Jean. (2000). "Despite Options on Census, Many to Check 'Black' Only." *New York Times.* February 12. Pp. A1, A9.

Senna, Danzy. (1998a). *Caucasia.* New York: Riverhead.

Senna, Danzy. (1998b). "The Mulatto Millennium." In O'Hearn, *Half + Half.* New York: Pantheon. Pp. 12–27.

Sollors, Werner. (1997). *Neither Black Nor White Yet Both: Thematic Explorations of Interracial Literature.* New York: Oxford University Press.

Spencer, Jon Michael. (1997). *The New Colored People: The Mixed-Race Movement in America.* New York: New York University Press.

Spencer, Rainier. (1999). *Spurious Issues: Race and Multiracial Identity Politics in the United States.* Boulder, CO: Westview.

Spickard, Paul. (1992). "The Illogic of American Racial Categories." In *Racially Mixed People in America,* ed. Maria P. P. Root. Newbury Park, CA: Sage. Pp. 12–23.

Spickard, Paul. (1999). Review of Werner Sollors, *Neither Black Nor White Yet Both,* and Jon Michael Spencer, *The New Colored People: The Mixed-Race Movement in America.* In *Journal of American Ethnic History.* 18.2. Pp. 153–56.

Spickard, Paul. (in press). "What's Critical About White Studies." In *Uncompleted Independence: Creating and Revising Racial Ideas in the United States,* ed. Spickard and G. Reginald Daniel. South Bend, IN: University of Notre Dame Press.

Spickard, Paul, and W. Jeffrey Burroughs, eds. (2000). *We Are a People: Narrative and Multiplicity in Constructing Ethnic Identity.* Philadelphia: Temple University Press.

Spickard, Paul, and Laurie Mengel. (1997). "Deconstructing Race: The Multiethnicity of Sui Sin Far." *Books and Culture.* November.

Stephens, Gregory. (1999). *On Racial Frontiers: The New Culture of Frederick Douglass, Ralph Ellison, and Bob Marley.* Cambridge: Cambridge University Press.

Talalay, Kathryn. (1995). *Composition in Black and White: The Life of Philippa Schuyler.* New York: Oxford University Press.

Thandeka. (1999). *Learning to be White: Money, Race, and God in America.* New York: Continuum.

Thompson, Becky, and Sangeeta Tyagi, eds. (1996). *Names We Call Home: Autobiography on Racial Identity.* New York: Routledge.

Tizard, Barbara, and Ann Phoenix. (1993). *Black, White, or Mixed Race? Race and Racism in the Lives of Young People of Mixed Parentage.* London: Routledge.

Van Tassell, M. Royce. (2000). "Americans Are Tired of Racial Boxes: Vast Majority Want Government to 'Leave My Race Alone!'" *The Egalitarian.* 3.2. Sacramento: American Civil Rights Institute. Pp. 1, 5.

Wallinger, Hanna. (in press). "Not Color but Character: Alice Dunbar-Nelson's Uncompleted Argument." In *Uncompleted Independence: Creating and Revising Racial Ideas in the United States,* ed. Paul Spickard and G. Reginald Daniel. South Bend, IN: University of Notre Dame Press.

West, Dorothy. (1995). *The Wedding.* New York: Doubleday.

Transition. (1996). *The White Issue.* Number 73.

White-Parks, Annette. (1995). *Sui Sin Far/Edith Maude Eaton.* Urbana: University of Illinois Press.

Williams, Gregory Howard. (1995). *Life on the Color Line: The True Story of a White Boy Who Discovered He Was Black.* New York: Penguin.

Williams-León, Teresa, and Cynthia Nakashima, eds. (2001). *The Sum of Our Parts: Mixed-Heritage Asian Americans.* Philadelphia: Temple University Press.

Wray, Matt, and Annalee Newitz, eds. (1997). *White Trash: Race and Class in America.* New York: Routledge.

Zack, Naomi. (1993). *Race and Mixed Race.* Philadelphia: Temple University Press.

Zack, Naomi, ed. (1995). *American Mixed Race.* Lanham, MD: Rowman and Littlefield.

"MY FATHER? GABACHO?" ETHNIC DOUBLING IN GLORIA LOPEZ STAFFORD'S *A PLACE IN EL PASO*

MARC CORONADO

UNIVERSITY OF CALIFORNIA, SANTA BARBARA

What personal attributes are necessary to sustain the choice to be known as multiracial or multiethnic? Making such a choice is seldom easy; if we choose to align ourselves with one part of our background, we risk alienating the people we need most—those in our own family or neighborhood. Psychological flexibility and a willingness to be open and compassionate to those who don't quite understand our decisions seem to be the most pronounced qualities that Gloria Lopez Stafford's 1996 memoir suggests. Although a hard protective shell may be the result of enduring and resisting life-long racial oppression, the resulting inflexibility also limits our ability to fully integrate the two worlds in which border dwellers must live. To build an effective and supportive multiethnic community, individuals must be involved in a process of constant nurturing, educating, building, and rebuilding.

The clash of hybrid geocultural identities has been the basis for Chicana/o narratives since long before the 1959 publication of the first Chicano novel, José Antonio Villarreal's *Pocho*. José David Saldivar traces the depiction of this cultural conflict back to Maria Amparo Ruiz de Burton's 1885 historical romance, *The Squatter and the Don*. And, certainly multiracial or multiethnic Chicana/o identity goes back even further than that, to the first sexual and social encounters of men and women from differing groups in the American borderlands.

In Chicana/o culture, these issues of identity construction, questions of cultural alchemy, and community acceptance or rejection based on ethnicity have been central to narrative for more than a hundred years. For Chicana/o writers in contemporary literature, these conflicts have almost always been posed as a Chicana/o "us" versus an Anglo "them," where the expression of Chicano/a culture as resistance and struggle has been opposed to the assumed coherence and consensus attributed to a dominant Anglo society.

This picture of cultural hostility changes when both "us" and "them" are merged and represented in a single subject. Our understanding of the cultural split shifts when the character represented by a text is Chicana as well as Anglo. In Gloria Lopez Stafford's memoir, *A Place in El Paso*, we come to know her as the child, Yoya, and the author portrays her younger self as an individual with a flexible and fluid ethnicity. In trying to understand her own ethnic identity, cultural traditions collide as well as intersect and interweave within a single person. In this memoir, cultural differences are not allowed to dissolve in a soothing movement toward consensus, and the multicultural moment is one of tension, struggle, discomfort, and disagreement. But this is simultaneously a moment of hope for fuller self-awareness, and for claiming a place in a multiethnic community. By adopting a willingness to know herself as a complex individual with a life embedded in an ethnically and culturally diverse community, Yoya is able to resist the presumption of an unproblematic "us" as well as to avoid falling into the trap of seeing all Anglos as an undifferentiated "them." What helps her to develop an understanding of her own complexity are her embrace of a dual cultural heritage and her willingness to open herself to the possiblities of change.

For Yoya, the position of the hybrid subject is never simply expressed by taking what is Anglo and what is Mexican and melding them harmoniously together in the creation of her own identity. Often she finds herself being one and then the other, or foregrounding one identity and backgrounding the other. This is a quality that Maria Root has called "ethnic shifting," developing the ability to transition from one ethnic identity to another without losing either a sense of self or allegiance to either ethnicity. For most of the text, the reader understands Yoya as a Mexican child living in the United States and dealing with the poverty of the barrio as well as the pressures to acculturate or to become

American. She grows up in a neighborhood where Spanish is the primary language, and the El Paso of the 1950s provides a backdrop in which speaking English is seldom necessary unless you're dealing with the State. Yoya speaks only Spanish fluently, and she's chastised for doing so, both in school by her teachers and at home by her father. He's afraid she'll be stopped when she crosses the border if she can't speak English to the Border Patrol. His fear is a very real one in a time and a culture where children crossed the border on foot without a parent, and carried no identification. Yoya doesn't see why she can't be an American and speak only Spanish or retain her Mexican culture. After all, she celebrates two independence days, the Fourth of July as well as the 16th of September. She bravely resists Americanization in the classroom as she cheers for the Mexicans during a showing of the film about the Alamo. In her home, she reads the Spanish language newspapers published in Juarez, *El Fronterizo* and *El Continental.* All of these everyday acts are symbolic of Mexican culture being preserved on the U.S. side of the border. To Yoya these contradictions are part of the way life is for a nine-year-old living in the borderlands.

The narrative of *A Place in El Paso* is complicated by Lopez Stafford's insertion of adult knowledge and adult feelings about ethnic doubling into the story of Yoya's life. Each chapter starts with an observation made by the adult narrator, and almost seamlessly glides into the world of Yoya through the use of dialogue. In one of the first chapters of the book, "The Second Ward," the narrator tells readers, "I call myself Mexican-American because I am both" (Lopez Stafford 8). Here Lopez Stafford is referring to herself, not to Yoya, who always calls herself Mexican. Part of this difference in nomenclature has to do with the history of ethnic naming on the border. In the 1940s and '50s few Mexicans or Chicana/os living in the U.S. referred to themselves by the hyphenated term, Mexican-American, that became popular during the Americanization movement of the later '50s and early '60s. Another influence on the name Lopez Stafford uses to describe her nationality is her adult acceptance of her doubled ethnicity. She goes on to explain that her Anglo father, of Swedish descent, married her Mexican mother in Piedras Negras, and that is where she was born. If we attribute ethnicity to birthplace or maternal lineage, she is Mexican. She entered El Paso as a U.S. citizen two years later because, Palm, her father, "was a norteamericano" (9). If we attribute ethnicity to migration or paternal lineage, she is American, or perhaps Swedish-Mexican-American.

As this story progresses we enter the world of the little girl who considers herself primarily Mexican. At age nine, Yoya is making salsa with a friend of the family. The narrator says, "I told Maria, 'Palm makes salsa on a food grinder and I help him turn the handle.'" Maria replies, "Yes, that is how Norteamericanos make it," and notices "a puzzled look" on Yoya's face. The child responds by asking if her father is "Gabacho?" The slang term for an Anglo and the child's confusion surprise Maria, who answers, "Seguro. What did you think your father was? And don't use that word, it is disrespectful." Yoya responds that she thought he was "Mexican, just like you and me" (117). Because her father speaks to her only in Spanish and has close ties to both family members and business acquaintances in Juarez, and because she grows up in El Paso's Segundo Barrio, where her neighbors, as the narrator explains, are "predominantly Spanish speaking, Mexican or U.S. citizens of Mexican descent," Yoya thinks of herself as well as her father as Mexican. Ideas of nationality mean something tangibly different to her than to the adults around her. For Yoya, Mexicanness is cultural. It's found in food eaten, customs preserved, stories told, holidays celebrated. For most of the adults in her life, Americanness means denying or supressing any other national affiliation.

The adult narrator of the memoir constantly reminds the reader of the child's doubled position—as both Mexican and American. Lopez Stafford also acts as linguistic translator for the reader. The narrator translates italicized Spanish words and phrases in the text into English immediately. The child's Spanish words and phrases, even complete sentences in dialogue are never translated. If we assume that as a memoir, *A Place in El Paso* is an account based on personal experience, this may be a mirror of the impact biculturalism has had on one woman's life. But it is also be representative of the larger phenomenon of biculturalism or multiculturalism. Yoya's experience is bicultural because it involves the process of subject creation where Mexican and U.S. border cultures collide. It is multicultural if we acknowledge the often forgotten truth that both Mexican and

U.S. cultures are in fact ethnically heterogeneous. Lopez Stafford describes the multiethnic borderlands of El Paso/Juarez by focusing on the complex history of migration that has helped to form the twin cities' unique ethnic makeup. She describes the Chinese merchants working at the mercado in Juarez, the Tarahumara Indians and the bigotry they encounter from the Mexican government, and the Spanish maestro who befriends Yoya and plays the "Polonaise" for her. She details the multilayered ethnic and cultural history of Spain, dominated in turn by a variety of Europeans as well as Moors and people from the Middle East. She also details the global immigrations to Mexico, including Africans, Asians and Pacific Islanders as well as Europeans. As she grows up, Yoya realizes that her school friends and her neighbors on the U.S. side of the border are Arab and Syrian, Irish, Czech, Polish and Greek as well as African-American and of multiple ethnic mixtures as well. Her description of El Paso/Juarez and the cosmopolitan nature of the symbiotic community that affects even the most economically impoverished of its members defies the often overworked image of the border town as a dusty, isolated place where life is divided into simplistic images of "us" and "them."

Such multiculturalism or doubled ethnicity is not painless, however, and an acute awareness of prejudice and disharmony is expressed by both the narrator and the child throughout the text. In a poignant moment in the schoolyard, twelve-year-old Yoya asks her school friend, Barbara, if she can "come and visit some afternoon after school" (195). She is told "no" and "not ever" because Barbara's mother does not want "any Mexican kids around." Yoya suggests that "You don't have to tell her I am Mexican," but her argument is countered with "the minute you open your mouth, she'll know you're Mexican" (195). Betrayed by her own voice and her original language, the child, stunned into silence, goes home and looks at her "[step]mother as I had never looked at her before. She was Mexican and a part of what I had always known. Somehow I was different than I had been two hours earlier" (196). Her desire to push her Mexican ethnicity into the background fails here, and the child realizes that ethnic choice is not always available to those of mixed backgrounds. To try to understand her sudden difference, Yoya considers the color of her skin and that of her family, she listens to bilingual chatter between them, she examines the freckles on her face. She asks her mother what makes someone American or Mexican, and finally seeks the counsel of her friend and priest Padre Luna.

When she asks the priest, "Am I Mexican or am I American?" he answers that she is both. "You have both bloods in you, and that will be a problem for you all your life if you let it" (203). The priest attributes Gloria's ethnicity to both biology, or blood, and to personal choice by concluding that she can control the degree to which racism affects her life. He explains to her that he was the child of Spanish immigrants to Mexico, but as an adult he "chose to see [him]self and call [him]self Mexican" because of his empathy for the poor he served through the Church. After a sensitive explanation of how prejudice is taught to children by parents and teachers, he encourages her to take control of the way she is treated by others. While it may be overly simplistic to believe that a twelve-year-old girl can entirely control how she is perceived, for Yoya the priest's speech is a challenge to acknowledge that she is doubled and enriched by her ethnic mix, and it is encouragement to attempt to control how she responds to bigotry. The priest may be an optimist, and of course, not everyone has the ability to control how he or she is seen. Those individuals who are at the bottom of the socioeconomic ladder are often perceived as whatever label is most despised by those in power. The victims of bigotry should not be held responsible for their own suffering; however, a strong sense of self and one's place in the fabric of the community does increase the possibility of responding to hate in a way that empowers rather than destroys the individual.

For months after the incident with Barbara, Yoya notices every reference to Mexicans or Anglos that anyone makes and eventually she decides the hurt of that one incident may never go away. The fact remains that she is both, Mexican and American, and she likes the combination because it "makes her whole." This sense of completeness may represent a coming to terms with the very nature of duality, and perhaps a part of the acceptance resides in the coming of age experience itself. Recognizing gender difference and our culture's expectatons of us as women often serves to help us define ourselves more clearly.

Gloria's gender position in this border zone may be part of what increases her personal flexibility and enables her to accept her doubled self as whole more readily. The border itself is often expressed by critics, novelists and journalists as a split, a wound, a tear, or a divide. Guillermo Gomez-Peña calls it a "fissure between two worlds" (101). Each of these terms has also been used historically as an essentializing symbol of the feminine. The myths abound. Woman was torn from Adam's side, Athena was born from the wound on Zeus' head, on and on the story goes that women are symbols of rupture. Chicano mythology has its own story of a divide attributed to a woman—it was La Malinche who fragmented indigenous civilization through her complicity with Europeans. Is there a way to re-form this essentialist representation as a positive rather than a negative factor for the bicultural, multiethnic subject and to use it strategically? Arlene Raven, an artist and writer in New York, who has called the U.S.–Mexico border a "wound," has written that "in order to heal the wound, we first have to open it" (qtd. in Peña 104). Opening oneself to another for change to occur and for love to take place may be part and parcel of being female, but it may also be as Gomez-Peña contends, "extremely painful and scary" (105). It is certainly not without consequence.

Gomez-Peña describes the way that Chicana/os "de-Mexicanized ourselves to Mexi-understand ourselves, some without wanting to, others on purpose" (101). As Renato Rosaldo and Saldivar have suggested before him, in Gomez-Peña's version of the story of Americanization something vital has been given up intentionally, or taken away by force in order for integration into otherness to take place. For men, castration anxiety is projected onto the Chicano warrior hero as he must de-Mexicanize himself to gain cultural understanding. Gomez-Peña continues the metaphor of the border as a rupture by asserting that "the borders either expand or are shot full of holes. Cultures and languages mutually invade one another" (102). The boundaries of perceived cultural purity and wholeness are penetrated by otherness, and in the intersection a new bicultural, multiethnic subject is born. These subjects are the border youth described by Gomez-Peña as those who "become the heirs to a new mestizaje," and a more profoundly articulated multiculturalism (102). For some Chicanos and Chicanas the most frightening part of this new mestizaje—represented by the even more hybrid, multiethnic, multicultural youth—is that he or she threatens a sense of ethnic equilibrium based on a fabricated image of Chicana/o racial purity—an "us" that is equally as racist and narrow minded as any unexamined Anglo "them."

Gomez-Peña recognizes that the dominant culture is a mirage that exists to control the everyday lives of individual subjects, and stresses that through the act of reading we are all border crossers. To survive we must learn to deal with openness, learn from the wounds and the ruptures of the border. Coming to terms with constant cultural intersections is inevitable in the transnational age, and we all are changed along the way.

In her memoir, Lopez Stafford writes that as an adolescent she decided to revel in the doubling of her ethnic and national identity. As the story ends, she tells a friend that she wants to marry a man who can "sing like a mariachi and dance the two-step like a Texan." She laughs and she shouts a loud "AyyAyyyAyyAyy!" like a Mexican vaquero (212). The narrator does not reenter the story at this point, but leaves the reader with the echo of the child's voice raised in celebration and hope for her Mexican American self, not a self halved by the division of ethnicities, but one doubled by the possibility of the acceptance of both. In *A Place in El Paso*, Lopez Stafford asks readers to consider whether the juxtaposition of cultures and ethnicities within one person necessarily causes a fractured personality or if instead, doubling can be seen instead as enrichment and addition. Her memoir suggests that psychic damage is not necessarily the result of cultural mestizaje, and this may have as much to do with the historical, ethnic, and geographical position of the author as it does with Yoya's cheerful optimism and openness to change.

The late 1990s, the time in which the author reflected on her life, represented a highly transnational moment for those living on the border. As Roger Rouse noted in his research on the lives of Mexican migrant workers in that decade, "the mobilization of modern socio-spatial images has become increasingly unable to contain the postmodern complexities that it confronts." Those people who are obliged to live within a transnational space, as all those who live on the border are, have become exponents of a cultural bifocality that defies reduction to a single order (Rouse 213). Lopez Stafford's memoir acknowledges that this ability to focus on multiplicity and develop attendant coping skills by living in the midst of cultural clash has existed for at least as long the U.S.–Mexican border itself. The intersections and the biculturalism are painful experiences and are not simple or simply resolved. As Gomez-Peña describes the clash of cultures, it is "a bitter split between two lovers from the same hometown," but the work that it takes to dismantle the mechanisms of fear can guide us to negotiate towards a peaceful coexistence and fruitful cooperation (101). The discontinuities of biculturalism and multiple ethnicity may be tears, wounds, or ruptures that we should not seek to close too quickly. The intransigence that identifies cultures, racial groups, and ethnicities as closed systems are much more dangerous than the spaces opened by the creative potential of acknowledging bicultural or multiethnic identity. It is time for all of us to consider what happens when their narratives and ours merge in this opening, and to listen to the multiethnic subject who acknowledges this position and uses it as a means to end the arbitrary divisions that keep human beings apart.

Works Cited

Gomez-Peña, Guillermo. "Excerpts from Warrior for Gringostroika." *The Late Great Mexican Border.* Eds. Bobby Byrd and Susannah Mississippi Byrd. El Paso: Cinco Puntos Press, 1997.

Lopez Stafford, Gloria. *A Place in El Paso: A Mexican American Childhood.* Albuquerque: U of New Mexico P, 1996.

Root, Maria. *The Multiracial Experience: Racial Borders as the New Frontier.* Thousand Oaks, California: Sage Publications, 1996.

Rosaldo, Renato. *Culture and Truth: The Remaking of Social Analysis.* Boston: Beacon Press, 1993.

Rouse, Roger. "Mexican Migration and the Social Space of Postmodernism." *Diaspora,* Spring 1991.

Saldivar, José David. *Border Matters: Remapping American Cultural Studies.* Berkeley: U of California P, 1997.

Burritos and Bagoong: Mexipinos and Multiethnic Identity in San Diego, California

Rudy P. Guevarra, Jr.

University of California, Santa Barbara

Introduction

In September of 1999, my cousin Selena had her first-year birthday party. My family and friends were gathered around in the backyard when the Mexican *trio* showed up to play at my aunt's house in Barrio Logan.[1] Ice-cold bottles of Corona and Pacifico were passed around while the musicians played. Some of us began dancing to the old Mexican *corridos* and *rancheros*, while others whistled and cheered us on with *gritos*.[2] The evening was progressing well when I noticed an odd expression on the faces of the musicians. They exchanged surprised looks as they saw the food being served to the guests. It was not the typical Mexican cuisine of *carne asada*, beans, salsa, and tortillas, but steamed rice, *lumpia, pansit,* and *pan de sal*. Nevertheless, they continued playing while we ate Filipino food and danced to the Mexican music.

This scene is familiar to me, one I have grown up with as a child. I always had the combination of Mexican and Filipino culture, food, and language around me. I would eat chicken *adobo* one day, only to eat *arroz con pollo* the next. My father and *tata* (grandfather) would tell me about my Filipino family, instilling a sense of pride, while my mother gave me that same sense of pride about my Mexican family and heritage. We had it all, rice and beans, tacos and lumpia, soy sauce and salsa. I knew that this was a combination that not everyone shared, yet it was so comfortable to me.

As a child growing up with this experience, I also thought of myself and my family as being unique. Besides my siblings and cousins, I grew up thinking that I was the only Mexican-Filipino, or *Mexipino*, among my peers.[3] My Mexican friends were amazed that I had Filipino in me, and my Filipino friends had no idea that I was half Filipino, because my physical features made me look more Mexican to them. I was always mistaken as just Chicano or Latino, until I made it known that I was also Filipino. Only then would people say to me, "Yeah, I can tell by your eyes," as if this physical marker were the only way I could be recognized as being Filipino. Growing up as a child, I was accepted by both sides and had a strong sense of who I am. As I went on to high school and college, I met other Mexipinos who had similar stories to my own. It was amazing to meet others who shared my thoughts and experiences. Another Mexipino friend of mine named Sonny always joked with me about his experience growing up, and how he was the only kid in his barrio that he knew of who ate burritos and *bagoong*.[4] Stories such as these reinforced the bond among this small group of my peers when we discussed childhood memories of family, culture, food, and religion.

As a rule, we all grew up in both cultures, knowing that we were Mexican and Filipino, Chicano and Pinoy.[5] It was an identity that we accepted with pride. We had no problem identifying with both cultures, because both were validated by our multiethnic families.[6] It was not something we questioned. As far as we were concerned, we did not have some of the problems that other multiethnic or multiracial individuals had in terms of identity issues and the experiences that shaped them.[7] In terms of my own experiences, I was able to "pass" between Mexican and Filipino communities, as well as other ethnic communities, where my identity was not seen as being Chicano or Latino, or even Filipino, but actually ambiguous in nature. This was the advantage that we saw in our identity as Mexipinos. We could pass as Middle Easterners, Polynesians, Greeks, American Indians, and other ethnic groups, because we were a group of individuals with a look, an experience, and an identity that res-onated with more than one culture. With regards to passing, we had few, if any boundaries or borders.[8] Little did we know that there was a significant number of Mexipino children like us in other areas of San Diego. As I grew up and spoke to more people, I found that this number was larger than I realized, but that our collective experiences were not recorded or known outside individual Mexipino communities.[9] In my exploration of Mexipino identity, I found out that I was not a first generation Mexipino, but a third generation. My father and grandmother were also Mexipinos, although they grew up identifying with their Filipino culture, thus they considered themselves Filipino.[10] It wasn't until I started asking questions, looking at old family photos, and questioning our family history that I found the long legacy of interethnic mixing occurring between Mexicans and Filipinos in San Diego. It was not only an experience my family had, but one that could possibly describe other families within the Mexican and Filipino communities of San Diego. Family stories perpetuated in these communities tell of a long history of interethnic relationships between Mexicans and Filipinos. But was this experience unique to San Diego, or even within my own family, or could this be a shared experience that others had? What could this tell us of the history of San Diego's Mexican and Filipino communities, as well as the history of the city in the larger context of its formation? In trying to answer some of these questions, I found that other communities besides San Diego also have Mexipino populations. These include, but are not limited to, Los Angeles, the San Joaquin Valley, the Bay Area, and the Imperial Valley. In these areas as well, there are Mexican and Filipino populations that live together in adjoining communities, attend the same Roman Catholic churches, work in the same labor force, and experience the same types of discrimination.

San Diego may be representative of other communities that have Mexipino children, but I will suggest that its experience is unique in its own right. The fact that San Diego was established as a military town, had large industries such as agriculture and fish canning, is close to Mexico, and is the third largest destination for contemporary Filipinos immigrants in the country, is primarily why Mexipino identity is dynamic and ongoing, spanning several generations.[11] San Diego is the ideal place for Mexipino identity to flourish and grow, as I will try to illustrate throughout this paper.

There have been previous studies on both the Mexican and

Filipino communities in San Diego as separate entities. These include an oral history of Filipinos in San Diego by Yen Le Espiritu (1995), a master's thesis on Filipino migrants in San Diego by Adelaida Castillo-Tsuchida (1979), and a history of Mexicans in nineteenth-century San Diego by Richard Griswold del Castillo and Manuel Hidalgo (1992).[12]

Yet none of these studies mentions the interactions of Mexicans and Filipinos, despite the fact that their communities often overlap. Similarly, other scholars such as Paul R. Spickard, have noted the lack of research that has been done on the inter-ethnic relationship between Mexicans and Filipinos.[13] In surveying secondary Asian American and Chicano Studies sources, I have noticed along with other scholars, that multiethnic or multiracial individuals and relationships are generally overlooked and marginalized by both fields.[14] It is not until recently that scholars in Asian American Studies have begun to recognize and include the experiences of multiethnic Asian Americans. Scholars in Chicano Studies have acknowledged multiethnicity among Mexicans and Chicanos, but limited their scope to the Indian-Spanish and Mexican-Anglo mixing that grew out of Spanish and American colonialism.[15] By reconstructing this comparative history of Mexican and Filipino communities, as well as their interactions, I hope to initiate dialogue which will recognize and explore the formation of Mexipino multiethnic identity. In order to do so, I searched for studies that could provide me with a model for exploring the idea of multiethnic identity from a standpoint that resonated with the Mexipino experience. It is my hope that I can tell this story and share the experiences of Mexipinos in San Diego and compare that with what has been done on the Punjabi-Mexican experience in the Imperial Valley of California.

Making Ethnic Choices: A Comparative Model

It wasn't until I read Karen Isaken Leonard's *Making Ethnic Choices: California's Punjabi Mexican Americans* (1992), that I considered what my own experiences meant, not only to myself as a person of Mexican and Filipino descent, but in the context of other multiethnic identities and the various factors that helped to define them.[16] Leonard examines the invention and reinvention of ethnic identity between two groups (Punjabis and Mexican Americans) within a local context (in this case, the Imperial Valley). She sees ethnicity as being created and transformed by social relations.[17] In doing so, Leonard looks at three aspects that form ethnic identity among Punjabi Mexican Americans, or as she sometimes labels them, *Mexican-Hindus.*[18] These include the formation of ethnic identity, gender power relationships, and ethnic identity, within and outside the family.[19]

As Leonard examines these factors, she places them in the context of multiple topics, such as marriages and children, male and female networks, conflict and love within marriages, the coming of age of the second generation, and political change and ethnic identity. She shows how the ethnic identities of Punjabi Mexican Americans are formed by not only historical factors, but personal experiences that shape who they are and how they identify themselves as multiethnic people. As she notes, "Their history can tell us a great deal about the historical construction of ethnicity and its meaning to people across time, space and context."[20]

Leonard's study raises fundamental questions regarding race and ethnic identity among Mexipinos. Are Mexipinos, like Punjabi Mexican Americans, a distinct group within or between the Chicano or Asian American community? How do our lives reflect not only the diversity of the Chicano and Asian American experience, but the formation of a multiethnic population that is fast becoming a reality for much of America? How do we, to quote Teresa Williams-Leon and Cynthia L. Nakashima, "challenge and redefine race and ethnicity, culture and community" within Asian American and Chicano Studies?[21] The experiences or "voices" of Mexipinos need to be heard, so that this growing phenomenon can be explained in the context of multiethnic and multiracial identity formation, especially with the "biracial baby boom" that began taking place after 1967.[22] To understand this phenomenon, the term *Mexipino* must be briefly explained.

Mexipino Identity

Language is the way in which we define ourselves and the world around us. It is a means to empower or oppress, and is important to the issue of race relations.[23] With regards to identity, language has always been reformed with the times to accommodate each varying generation and the terms they use to describe themselves. It is in this context that I use, and at times critique, language as a tool to validate, reevaluate, and form an identity, which is a central theme in my study of Mexipinos. As Maria Root suggests, language and self-designating are "important vehicles for self-empowerment of oppressed people. Labels are powerful comments on how one's existence is viewed."[24] By proclaiming the self-imposed label of *Mexipino*, I take this as a means of empowerment, much in the same way in which the term *Chicano* was used as a means to empower the Mexican American community of the 1960s and 1970s. And as the term Chicano had political connotations, so does the term Mexipino, for it acknowledges the multiethnic character of the individual. It is also a way of taking two familiar terms, Mexican and Filipino, and transforming them into a new concept, *Mexipino*.[25] This new term states that multiethnicity must be addressed and recognized, for it has always been a part of the human character and a growing phenomenon in the U.S., which was recently recognized by the 2000 census. Such recognition is necessary to empower those who do not see themselves as a sum of parts, but as whole persons who embody all aspects of their identity.[26]

For those of us who are familiar with the term, we use *Mexipino* to define ourselves, rather than being defined by others.[27] It is our way of distinguishing the multiethnic identity of people who are of Mexican and Filipino descent. We use the term as a single word to note that even though we are comprised of two separate ethnicities, we are one individual who embodies both aspects of our Mexican and Filipino cultures.[28] Although there have been other terms used by others of this mixed heritage, such as *Chicapino, Chicaflip, Mexiflip, Flipsican,* or *fish taco,* among other terms, I contend that Mexipino is a more inclusive and positive self-defining term.[29] *Chicapino* is used by more contemporary Mexican-Filipinos, yet *Mexipino* describes not only my generation, born in the late 1960s and early 1970s during the "biracial baby boom," but previous generations. These previous generations did not use the term *Chicano*, but *Mexican*. Because the term *Mexican* is for the most part acknowledged and accepted by various generations, I feel that *Mexipino* is intergenerational for those who are multiethnic of Mexican and Filipino descent.

Other terms, such as *Mexiflip, Chicaflip,* and *fish taco,* among others, although used by us as a means of joking about our identity with each other, do have negative connotations when used by those who are non-Mexican or non-Filipino. The term "flip" is used as a derogatory word to describe Filipinos. The same can be said of "fish taco," if one chooses to use it in a derogatory way. Thus, the term that I contend is most appropriate, as well as most inclusive of all generations of multiethnic Mexican-Filipinos, is *Mexipino.* In addition, it is a term that is familiar not only to my friends and me, but among some of the other Mexipinos whom I have interviewed in San Diego. It is an inclusive term that describes not only who we are as a multiethnic group, but our experiences, the history behind our identity, and what makes our experience unique. Not only do we redefine who we are in terms of our multiplicity, but we redefine and challenge existing notions of what it means to be a Mexican or Chicano, Filipino or Pinoy.

Using Leonard's model of Punjabi Mexican Americans as a starting point to discuss Mexipino multiethnicity, I argue that Mexicans and Filipinos differ from other multiethnic and multiracial communities, as well as from Leonard's study of Punjabi Mexican Americans, in several ways. First, San Diego Mexicans and Filipinos have a mutual understanding of each other because of their common history of conquest by Spanish colonists and their culture, language, and Catholic religion.[30] In addition, they share common interests and purposes through the bonds of intermarriages, family and extended family relations, kinship networks, and *compradazgo,* or god-parenthood.

Through these mutual and shared experiences, Mexicans and Filipinos in San Diego developed an inclusive relationship much different from Leonard's study, which contributed to the development and growth of the Mexipino community. This interrelationship has been sustained by the proximity of San Diego to Mexico, resulting in substantially large numbers of Mexicans settling in the city, and by the fact that nation's second largest Filipino population resides in San Diego.[31] These factors, I contend, continue to have an impact on the perpetual growth of Mexipinos in San Diego, thus making this phenomenon transcend several generations. Several factors besides immigration experiences also contributed to the common historical bonds of

Mexicans and Filipinos: the repatriations during the Great Depression; racial segregation and discrimination, which confined community development in specific areas as a result of restricted covenants; and racial violence during World War II, such as the "zoot suit" conflicts instigated by Navy and Army personnel.[32]

I suggest that all of these shared experiences contributed to the development of the relationships between Mexicans and Filipinos, thus providing opportunities for love and marriage, and eventually children. These Mexipino children are manifestations of a historical legacy that continues to shape and mold their multiethnic identity as they come of age during the twentieth and twenty-first centuries—and transcend the boundaries of race and ethnicity.

Interviewing Other Mexipinos

In order to illustrate my experiences as a Mexipino in the larger context of growing up in a multiethnic community within San Diego, I interviewed other Mexipinos as further evidence for my research. All of my interviewees except one were from San Diego.[33] I interviewed one other Mexipino who was from a different area in Southern California, yet this experience in terms of identity and multiethnicity was similar to those I interviewed from San Diego. What I found was that we all shared three aspects of our identity, which other scholars, such as Maria Root, have identified among multiethnics.[34] These include the "best of both worlds" ideal, "ambiguous identity," and a related topic, "multiple passing." By sharing the stories of other Mexipinos, I hope to provide a context in which multiethnicity is defined, redefined, and even transformed by individuals of multiple ancestries.[35] With my research I have produced some concepts, although similar to previous research on multiethnic and multiracial individuals; nevertheless, these ideas have themselves been borrowed and redefined to explain the Mexipino experience in San Diego:

"Best of Both Worlds"

One of the common perceptions of those interviewed always addressed the idea that they had the "best of both worlds." It is a similar idea to what Christine C. Iijima Hall shares in her article on Black-Japanese biracial individuals.[36] Although she defines this term based on physical traits, I contend that Mexipinos share the "best of both worlds" on multiple levels, not just with regards to body image. Whether it was the cultural similarities of food, family, or childhood experiences, Mexipinos had a positive experience for the most part in understanding what it meant to be multiethnic and multicultural. As one interviewee noted:

> I was exposed to both cultures, and I don't think I would choose to live any other way because I had the best of both worlds. My dad was a cook, my mom was a cook. My dad cooked the best of the Filipino food that you can offer and my mom cooked the best Mexican food. Everyday it was something different... I wouldn't change my background for the world. I'm totally happy from where I am now to growing up. I would change a lot of things that I've done, but as far as having regrets for being who I am or my race, heck no. I'm proud of being Mexican and Filipino.[37]

His ideas of having the best of everything, be it food, family, and experiences growing up, illustrate the shared connectedness that Mexicans and Filipinos have, and the environment these two culture provide for their children. Because both sides share a Spanish colonial past, there seems to be the tendency for both groups to share many things that make the Mexipino experience unique. Among two of the most talked about aspects to this have been family and food. First, because family and extended family are central to both Mexican and Filipino life, there is one more aspect in which both groups can foster a familiar environment that produces positive childhood experiences. Second, food defines for many of the Mexipinos interviewed how both cultures go together and share in a common experience. For many of them, it is a unique experience that defines who they are. As one interviewee pointed out to me regarding family:

> Family does play a big issue; I think especially for me and my brother... family is the biggest thing. It's so nice to know that there's always a place you can go regardless. I'm never afraid of not living with someone because there is always a relative there. I think Mexicans and Filipinos have this big thing on family, and it's cool.[38]

Similarly, another interviewee shared her views on the importance of family in regards to culture, religion, and tradition. As she sees it:

> I guess the traditions are very close, the backgrounds are very close … I guess I see a closeness in regards to the traditions and family being, it should be, number one in your life always. That's what we were taught growing up, and then religion being important. I guess that's it, being a tighter family unit.[39]

For many Mexipinos, food reinforced family ties and traditions by sharing the tastes of both cultures and giving an opportunity to bring new experiences together in a setting that fostered this union. Food always makes an occasion that much more enjoyable, and as one interviewee shared, "the Filipinos love Mexican food and the Mexicans love Filipino food, so you know they will want the taco and the lumpia."[40] Others shared similar experiences:

> When we have parties, both the Mexican and Filipino sides of our families get together. There are a lot of people there! Our food is a combination of Mexican and Filipino. We have tortillas, beans, salsa, nopales, as well as lumpia, rice, pan de sal, and sandwiches. It's great![41]

Many of the interviewees also noted having the best of both worlds was that growing up with a multiethnic experience made them more open and accepting of other individuals and cultures. This made sense because of the fact that growing up in a multiethnic environment that was for the most part positive, provided them with an experience that enabled them to see two different, yet similar cultures coming together and laying the foundations for positive ethnic relations within the home. No aspect of their ethnic identity was better than the other, so this gave them the personal experience that they or anybody else were not inferior mentally, physically, or culturally.[42] Thus, their background was conducive for allowing Mexipinos to be more open and accepting to other cultures and ethnicities. As one interviewee stated:

> Our Mexipino culture is unique. Our cultures are so similar. We may deal with some prejudice, but there is a lot more understanding between the two cultures. Being Mexipino

also opens us up to learning about other people's cultures, and who people are because of what they are. It helps us to associate well with others. It is much different than a black and white racial mix (like my friend), where the two sides are played against each other culturally. It is not like that with us.[43]

Similarly, another interviewee noted that being Mexipino and the experiences that were associated with this identity allowed for more openness to other cultures. As she put it:

I think being Mexipino is a total advantage ... you just become so open minded and I notice, and with a lot of other people that are mixed, you're not just open minded to both Mexican and Filipino, but everyone. I think you become open minded to everything and you see and become attracted to other people. So I love being like this. I just think it makes you open minded to other people and cultures.[44]

Having family and food in the context of a multiethnic experience in the lives of Mexipinos are just some of the points that make their identity not only positive, but unique in many ways. It enabled them to grow up with an open mind, thus being willing to interact and experience other people and cultures. The other aspects of Mexipino identity found in common include the issues of identity and naming.

"Ambiguous Identity"

Often times Mexipinos are in the state of "ambiguous identity," that is to say, their physical traits, which normally would be associated with a certain racial group, are blurred by their multiplicity. Maria Root deals with this issue in a similar way with her notion of physical ambiguity with regards to people of multiethnic or multiracial backgrounds by her analysis of the ways in which identity is negotiated and redefined.[45] As most of the interviewees noted (and my own experiences illustrate), the common question of "What are you?" followed them throughout their lives. As Teresa Williams-Leon notes, "It assumes your foreignness and non-belonging for individuals whose identity is ambiguous." One's appearance does not fit the outsider's expectation of what a Mexican or Filipino is supposed to look like.[46]

Although Mexipinos neither completely (nor stereotypically)

fit the image of what a Mexican or Filipino is supposed to look like, often times people still are not quite sure what to make of them when they meet. According to some of my interviewees, as well as my own experiences, it is common that people often say "you look Mexican but ..." or, "you look like you're Filipino but you have ..." It is not uncommon for any individual who is multiracial or multiethnic, yet among multiethnic or multiracial Asian Americans, it is a situation that occurs at least on a weekly basis, as one interviewee noted.[47] A common thing for all of the people I interviewed was the "What are you?" question because their identity was ambiguous to the outsider.[48] As one interviewee stated:

> You really have to look at somebody and think okay, he's probably Filipino but then you probably have to be around a bunch of Filipinos to understand though because Filipinos have a distinct look. They don't look like other Asians because they are Pacific Islanders as well. People think I look more Mexican, although I think it's more because of the way I carry myself, rather than how I look.[49]

This leads to the next item that most Mexipinos deal with in regards to ambiguous identity, and that is the issue of being mistaken for another ethnicity, or the ability to pass into other ethnic communities. It is an issue that Maria Root also addresses in her concept of "both feet in both groups," even in groups not associated with the individual's race or ethnicity, when dealing with multiethnic or multiracial people.[50] It is for Root a multiple construction, but I contend that it results in what I call "multiple passing," where the individual can easily pass and blend in and out of their cultures and ethnicities, as well as others not associated with their background. This ability to transcend one's own physical appearance and outsider expectations is the result of multiple passing.

"Multiple Passing"

As stated previously, because of the ambiguous identity of Mexipinos, they often pass as other ethnicities or races, thus finding themselves in what Maria Root calls "situational ethnicity."[51] Yet for Mexipinos, situational ethnicity can be by choice or imposition from an outsider. Their physical characteristics enable them to pass not only within the Mexican and Filipino communities, but as I have noted through my own experiences, within other ethnic communities. As stated before, this ranges from Polynesian, Middle Eastern, Greek, and other multiethnic or racial groups. Mexipinos have been able to pass into various communities and even hold "honorary membership" in these groups because their physical features are much like other group members. As one Mexipino noted:

> Every person on the street asks me if I'm Persian. Like last year, I was approached by some Persians to join their club. They asked, "Are you Persian?" I said no, yet they still asked if I wanted to join their club. I said, "I'm not even Persian," and they were like, "It doesn't matter, just come." I think because I looked Persian that they still wanted me to be a part of their group.[52]

For the most part, what I've noticed is that among my Mexipino interviewees, they have often been mistaken as Polynesian. For example, one of my interviewees grew up being mistaken for Samoan. As she remembered:

> When I was little I had real long hair, my nose was pudgier, so people thought I was Samoan because of my mixed thing. Even my friend, who was also Samoan, thought I was one of them. I don't know if it's because of my mix, but I've also been mistaken for being Hawaiian.[53]

Other interviewees also notice that they or another of their siblings have been mistaken for being Hawaiian.[54] For others, they could blend right into the Mexican or Filipino communities. As one of my interviewees noted:

> Because I'm kind of dark I blended right in with the locals in Hawaii. I can also go to a Filipino party and blend right in with them and hang out. Same thing when I go down to Mexico, I blend right in there as well.[55]

In listening to their stories, I saw the connection of the experience as not only having to do with physical appearance, but location, which can add to the phenomenon of multiple passing. Whether in Mexico or a Mexican community in the U.S., the Mexipino's Mexican features seemed to be reinforced. It also was a similar experience with the Filipino side to this identity. Within my own experiences, and those of other Mexipinos I interviewed, when we were in Hawaii, we were mistaken as a "local."[56] Again, this was situational ethnicity based on location. The connecting thread in all this was that because one could pass into other communities and cultures, it often exposed Mexipinos to other experiences with these cultures that reinforced their ability to be more open to multiple ways of looking at multiplicity within individuals. It was again for the most part a positive experience that most of the interviewees had, or at least recognized. As I continue my research on Mexipino identity and gather more sources, I hope to provide a better picture of multiethnic identity, as well as the Mexican and Filipino communities in the larger context of the formation of San Diego as a major metropolitan city.

Conclusion

Throughout my paper I have suggested that the Mexipino experience in San Diego is unique in various ways. Multiethnic identity, which is challenged, redefined, and even transformed by Mexipinos, suggests that we must look at new ways of interpreting not only ethnic and race relations, but self identity. The experiences of those I interviewed shared a lot of common experiences, which included having the best of both worlds, ambiguous identity, and multiple passing. Through the connections of immigration, wage labor experiences, community formation, and a shared Spanish colonial past, among other things, laid the foundations for what would become a situation where interrelationships and bonds could be formed between the two groups. The similarities and shared aspects of family, food, and other cultural experiences, Mexicans and Filipinos have continued to form intimate relationships and intermarry through several generations, laying the foundations for the perpetual rise of Mexipinos in San Diego. It is an experience that is unique and embraced by those who share this multiethnic identity.

It must be noted that, as all relationships are concerned, none are perfect. My study and exploration into Mexipino identity is not to say that this is a perfect relationship. On the contrary, as with all relationships, be they interethnic or interracial, there are tensions that cannot be avoided. Be it economic, political, or social competition and animosity, all human relationships have their problems. Prejudice even exists within the Mexican-Filipino relationship. What some of the interviewees noted was that because they were mixed, some had more Mexican or Filipino features, even though they were accepted, their identity did at times come into question by either side of their ethnic background. At times they were even made fun of because of their multiplicity. Their identity would come into question based on their physical appearance.[57] As one of the interviewees recalls:

> The Mexicans thought you were too "Oriental" and the Filipinos thought you were too Mexican. If you didn't know Spanish, they (the Mexicans) would make fun of you, and if you didn't know Tagalog, they (the Filipinos) would make fun of you too. It was hard because I had friends in both cultures and all that, but it wasn't easy all the time because you were called half-breed or some other stupid remarks.[58]

A similar experience of questioning identity also occurred with another individual who stated:

> When I was little and playing with my cousins, I would be singled out like, "She doesn't look Filipino at all." It made me feel weird. They (relatives) would seriously sit there and study me, and just compare me to my brother and how come we didn't look alike, since he was more Filipino looking... even now I kind of get upset because now that I'm older why do I have to prove myself? Why do I have to look a certain way? This is who I am and I'm very secure with myself.[59]

These examples suggest that there are still some problems within the Mexican and Filipino communities in terms with identity. As it also has its flaws, the good in this relationship, I suggest, outweighs any other problems. As one of my other interviewees pointed out, within the larger context, and in general, if Mexicans and Filipinos (that lived in separate areas) knew their similarities, like those that lived in adjoining communities and had constant contact with each other (as is the case in San Diego), they would be more inclined to come together. She made a point by sharing this experience:

> I used to work in San Ysidro, and I talked to this Mexican man one day about politics. As I was speaking to him, I also began to talk to others in Spanish. He was very

surprised about this. He saw me at first as some stupid "China" until we talked. He then had respect for me and felt ashamed about the way he felt. He learned from me.[60]

What I suggest through these examples is that although the relationship is not perfect, it is more conducive for forming such interethnic ties and bonds, because of the understanding of each other's culture and the other factors I have mentioned. Because Mexicans and Filipinos share common bonds of culture, wage labor experiences, etc. in San Diego more than in other places, and because they do form interethnic relationships and mix, this recognition of their shared experiences are more profound.

This is why I contend that San Diego's Mexipino experience is unique. Not only does this experience span several generations, but it is a continual process. Both my niece and nephew are fourth-generation Mexipinos in San Diego, and as the two communities continue to live, work, and form relationships together, this will continue to occur because of the common experiences at the local, and even intimate level. Love has no boundaries, and in a situation where religion, cultural practices, and love of family exist, it will bring two people together to create a new experience that is unique; one where the children will not only redefine ethnic and racial borders, but provide a new way in which to see the world.

Bibliography

Primary Sources

U.S. Bureau of the Census. *Census 2000 Summary File 1 of the United States.* Prepared by the Bureau of the Census. Washington, D.C., 2001. <http://www.census.gov>.

Secondary Sources

Anzaldúa, Gloria. *Borderlands/La Frontera: The New Mestiza.* San Francisco: Aunt Lute Books, 1987.

Barrera, Mario, and Marilyn Mulford, prods. *Chicano Park.* San Diego: Redbird Films, 1988.

Bonus, Rick. *Locating Filipino Americans: Ethnicity & The Cultural Politics of Space.* Philadelphia: Temple University Press, 2000.

Castillo-Tsuchida, Adelaida. "Filipino Migrants in San Diego, 1900–1946." Master's thesis, University of San Diego, 1979.

Espiritu, Yen Le. *Filipino American Lives.* Philadelphia: Temple University Press, 1995.

Garcia, Ignacio M. *Chicanismo: The Forging of a Militant Ethos among Mexican Americans.* Tucson: University of Arizona Press, 1997.

Gaskin, Pearl Fuyo. *What Are You?: Voices of Mixed-Race Young People.* New York: Henry, Holt and Company, 1999.

Griswold del Castillo, Richard, and Manuel Hidalgo, eds. *Chicano Social and Political History in the Nineteenth Century.* Encino, California: Floricanto Press, 1992.

Hall, Christine C. Iijima. "Best of Both Worlds: Body Image and Satisfaction of a Sample of Black-Japanese Biracial Individuals." *Amerasia Journal,* Vol. 23, No.1 (1997): 87–97.

Houston, H. Ricka. "Between Two Cultures: A Testimony." *Amerasia Journal,* Vol. 23, No. 1 (1997): 149–154.

Johnson, Kevin R. *How Did You Get to be Mexican?: A White/Brown Man's Search for Identity.* Philadelphia: Temple University Press, 1999.

Kitano, Harry H. L., and Roger Daniels. *Asian Americans: Emerging Minorities.* Englewood Cliffs: Prentice Hall, 1995.

Leonard, Karen Isaken. *Making Ethnic Choices: California's Punjabi Mexican Americans.* Philadelphia: Temple University Press, 1992.

Menchaca, Martha. *Recovering History, Constructing Race: The Indian, Black, and White Roots of Mexican Americans.* Austin: University of Texas Press, 2001.

McReynolds, Patricia Justiani. *Almost Americans: A Quest for Dignity; An American Memoir.* Santa Fe: Red Crane Books, 1997.

Nash, Gary B. "The Hidden History of Mestizo America." In Martha Hodes, ed., *Sex, Love, Race: Crossing Boundaries in North American History.* New York: New York University Press, 1999, 10–32.

Posadas, Barbara M. *The Filipino Americans.* Westport, Connecticut: Greenwood Press, 1999.

Root, Maria P. P., ed. *Filipino Americans: Transformation and Identity.* Thousand Oaks, California: Sage Publications, 1997.

————, ed. *The Multiracial Experience: Racial Borders as the New Frontier.* Thousand Oaks, California: Sage Publications, 1996.

————, ed. *Racially Mixed People in America.* Newbury Park, California: SagePublications, 1992.

————. "The Multiracial Experience: Racial Borders as a Significant Frontier in Race Relations." In Maria P. P. Root, ed. *The Multiracial Experience: Racial Borders as the New Frontier.* Thousand Oaks, California: Sage Publications, 1996, xiii–xxviii.

Sanchez, George J. *Becoming Mexican American: Ethnicity, Culture and Identity in Chicano Los Angeles, 1900–1945.* New York: Oxford University Press, 1993.

Spickard, Paul, and W. Jeffrey Burroughs, eds. *We Are a People: Narrative and Multiplicity in Constructing Ethnic Identity.* Philadelphia: Temple University Press, 2000.

Spickard, Paul R. *Mixed Blood: Intermarriage and Ethnic Identity in Twentieth-Century America.* Madison: University of Wisconsin Press, 1989.

_____. "What Must I Be?: Asian Americans and the Question of Multiethnic Identity." *Amerasia Journal,* Vol. 23, No. 1 (1997): 44–60.

_____. "The Illogic of American Racial Categories," in Maria P. P. Root, ed., *Racially Mixed People in America.* Newbury Park, California: Sage Publications, 1992, 12–23.

_____. "Who is Asian? Who is Pacific Islander?: Monoracialism, Multiracial People, and Asian American Communities." In Teresa Williams-Leon and Cynthia L. Nakashima, eds. *The Sum of Our Parts: Mixed Heritage Asian Americans.* Philadelphia: Temple University Press, 2001, 13–24.

Villa, Dario Deguzman. *The Bridge Generation: Sons and Daughters of Filipino Pioneers.* San Diego: Dario D. Villa, 1996.

Williams-Leon, Teresa, and Cynthia L. Nakashima, eds. *The Sum of Our Parts: Mixed Heritage Asian Americans.* Philadelphia: Temple University Press, 2001.

Williams-Leon, Teresa. "Race as Process: Reassessing the 'what are you?' Encounters of Biracial Individuals." In Maria P. P. Root, ed., *The Multiracial Experience: Racial Borders as the New Frontier.* Thousand Oaks, California: Sage Publications, 1996, 191–210.

Zhou, Min, and James V. Gatewood, eds., *Contemporary Asian America: A Multidisciplinary Reader.* New York: New York University Press, 2000.

Interviews

Dixon, Jennifer. Interview by author. San Diego, Calif., 29 December 2001.

Fernandez, Susana. Interview by author. San Diego, Calif., 30 December 2001.

Limjoco, Sophia. Telephone interview with author, 8 January 2002.

Mariscal, Marissa. Interview by author. Santa Barbara, Calif., 8 February 2002.

Ochoa-Tafoya, Rachael. Interview by author. Santa Barbara, Calif., 5 January 2002.

Soliven, Dale. Interview by author. San Diego, Calif., 28 December 2001.

Notes

1. Barrio Logan is one of the oldest, and was at one time, one of the largest Mexican communities in San Diego, California. It is most recognized for its murals, located in Chicano Park, which has recently been deemed a historical landmark for the struggles that occurred between local Mexican residents and the city over a contested piece of land in their barrio. The result was the creation of a park in the image that the community wanted. For more on Barrio Logan and Chicano Park, see Mario Barrera and Marilyn Mulford, prods., *Chicano Park* (San Diego: Redbird Films, 1988). *Trios* are Mexican street musicians who hang around local restaurants and other areas in the barrio, and get hired to play at various residential and community celebrations.

2. *Gritos* are long, harmonious yells that Mexicans express while listening to music or showing their approval and excitement at a significant moment.

3. Another friend I interviewed had the same feeling growing up in San Diego. He also thought of himself as unique. He did not think that there were any other individuals with the same Mexican-Filipino heritage. It wasn't until he got older that he met others, and like my own experiences, saw a unique lifestyle and identity that was present in San Diego. See Dale Soliven, interview by author, San Diego, Calif., 28 December 2001.

4. *Bagoong* is a salty relish-like sauce that is made out of small fish or shrimp.

5. The term *Chicano* is very complex in its meaning. It can be used to identify Mexicans who are born in the United States, but can also be a state of consciousness and awareness: a political term to reflect resistance to the norm of identification that the government has placed upon Mexican Americans. It was a term adopted by the Chicano Movement as a means of resistance, which had its roots among the working class Mexican American population at the time. It is interesting to know that it was once thought of as a pejorative term. For this purpose, the term Chicano will refer to individuals who are born in the United States. The term Mexican will be used to identify those who are Mexican nationals, as well as Mexican Americans who also identify with just the term Mexican. Filipinos use the term *Pinoy* as self-identification, from the first wave of immigrants who came to the continental United States. It is currently used by Filipinos as a term of self-identification and pride, similar to how Chicanos identify themselves. Its original meaning also had pejorative connotations. In regards to this paper I will use the terms Filipino, Mexipino (see later description in paper for use of the term), and Chicano in the singular form to include both masculine and feminine form of the words. It is not my intention to exclude the feminine aspect to these terms, but for all intents and purposes, it is a lot less confusing to use the singular term, rather than repeatedly use both masculine and feminine forms for each term throughout the paper. For more specific

use of the terms mentioned, see Harry H. L. Kitano and Roger Daniel's *Asian Americans: Emerging Minorities* (Englewood Cliffs: Prentice Hall, 1995), p. 94; George J. Sanchez, *Becoming Mexican American: Ethnicity, Culture and Identity in Chicano Los Angeles, 1900–1945* (New York: Oxford University Press, 1993), pp. 7–14; Ignacio M. Garcia, *Chicanismo: The Forging of a Militant Ethos among Mexican Americans* (Tucson: University of Arizona Press, 1997), pp. 68–85; Maria P. P. Root, ed., *Filipino Americans: Transformation and Identity* (Thousand Oaks, California: Sage Publications, Inc.), pp. 95–111;and Barbara M Posadas, *The Filipino Americans* (Westport: Greenwood Press, 1999), p. 13.

6. I use the term *ethnic* over *racial* in illustrating my point on multi-ethnic identity because although the term "Mexican" was once considered a "racial" category, nonetheless it is an ethnic group, as are Filipinos (who were considered of the "Malay" race). The use of "ethnicity" and "race" also has various uses and meanings, depending on the context in which it is used. For more on the use the terms ethnic and race, see Paul Spickard and W. Jeffrey Burroughs, Eds., *We Are a People: Narrative and Multiplicity in Constructing Ethnic Identity* (Philadelphia: Temple University Press, 2000).

7. For examples of identity search and/or crisis of multiethnic children of Mexican and Filipino descent, see Patricia Justiani McReynold's *Almost Americans: A Quest for Dignity; An American Memoir* (Santa Fe: Red Crane Books, 1997) and Kevin R. Johnson, *How Did You Get to be Mexican?: A White/Brown Man's Search for Identity* (Philadelphia: Temple University Press, 1999).

8. For more on crossings between racial and ethnic "borders," see Maria P. P. Root, "The Multiracial Experience: Racial Borders as a Significant Frontier in Race Relations" in her ed., *The Multiracial Experience: Racial Borders as the New Frontier* (Thousand Oaks, California: Sage Publications, 1996), pp. xiii–xxviii; and Gloria Anzaldúa, *Borderlands/La Frontera: The New Mestiza* (San Francisco: Aunt Lute Books, 1987).

9. Although I have not collected a significant number of oral interviews with other Mexipinos to date, because this research project is a recent endeavor, I intend on conducting more interviews and obtaining actual demographic statistics based on my findings as my research progresses.

10. Among Mexipinos of my generation I noticed that even though we were raised in both Mexican and Filipino cultures, the Mexican side tended to be more dominant. I suggest that this is because for the most part we were raised by our mothers, who happened to be the Mexican individual in this relationship, and were the main providers for our cultural upbringing. I must note however that not all of the mothers of the interviewees I spoke with were Mexican. I am currently looking into the matter as to why my father and grandmother identified more with their Filipino, as opposed to their Mexican culture, and why their identity was either/or, and not both while growing up.

11. Yen Le Espiritu, *Filipino American Lives* (Philadelphia: Temple University Press, 1995), p. 22.

12. Ibid. See also Adelaida Castillo-Tsuchida, *Filipino Migrants in San Diego, 1900–1946* (M.A. Thesis: University of San Diego, 1979); Richard Griswold del Castillo and Manuel Hidalgo, eds., *Chicano Social and Political History in the Nineteenth Century* (Encino, California: Floricanto Press, 1992).

13. Paul R. Spickard mentions Karen Leonard's work on Punjabi-Mexican Americans, while at the same time recognizing that the Filipino community always had mixed couples and multiethnic children. It is within this context that he addresses the fact that the Filipino and Mexican relationship has not been explored. For more on this see Paul R. Spickard, "Who is Asian? Who is Pacific Islander?: Monoracialism, Multiracial People, and Asian American Communities," in Teresa Williams-Leon and Cynthia L. Nakashima, eds., *The Sum of Our Parts: Mixed Heritage Asian Americans* (Philadelphia: Temple University Press, 2001), pp. 16–17.

14. Paul Spickard notes in his article "What Must I Be?: Asian Americans and the Question of Multiethnic Identity" that the voices of multiethnic Asian Americans are often excluded from Asian American Studies. I also found similar trends in Chicano Studies, which does not include the voices of multiethnic Chicano/as as part of the Chicano/a experience. See Min Zhou and James V. Gatewood, eds., *Contemporary Asian America: A Multidisciplinary Reader* (New York: New York University Press, 2000), pp. 606–623; Williams-Leon and Nakashima, eds., *The Sum of our Parts*, p. 71.

15. Some of the fairly recent research that has been done on multi-ethnic and multiracial Asian Americans include studies such as Teresa Williams-Leon and Cynthia L. Nakashima, eds., *The Sum of Our Parts: Mixed Heritage Asian Americans* (Philadelphia: Temple University Press, 2001); a compilation of various articles in Amerasia Journal, Vol. 23, No. 1, (1997); Maria P. P. Root, ed., *The Multiracial Experience: Racial Borders as the New Frontier* (Thousand Oaks, California: Sage Publications, 1996); Root, ed., *Racially Mixed People in America* (Newbury Park, California: Sage Publications, 1992). The multiethnic and multira-cial experience has even less scholarship within Chicano Studies. Some of the scholarship that I found, didn't always fit under the umbrella of Chicano Studies (rather Ethnic Studies), but nevertheless had relative significance to the discipline. This includes Martha Menchaca, *Recovering History, Constructing Race: The Indian, Black, and White Roots of Mexican Americans* (Austin: University of Texas Press, 2001); Gary B. Nash, "The Hidden History of Mestizo America," in Martha Hodes, ed., *Sex, Love, Race: Crossing Boundaries in North American History* (New York: New York University Press, 1999).

16. Karen Isaken Leonard, *Making Ethnic Choices: California's Punjabi Mexican Americans* (Philadelphia: Temple University Press, 1992).

17. Ibid., p. 12.

18. Ibid., p. x.

19. Ibid., p. 13.

20. Ibid., p. 14.

21. Williams-Leon and Nakashima, eds., *The Sum of our Parts*, p. 6.

22. Ibid., p. 5; Root, ed., *The Multiracial Experience*, p. xv.

23. Root, *The Multiracial Experience*, p. xxiv.

24. Ibid., p. xxiii.

25. Ibid., p. xxiv.

26. Williams-Leon and Nakashima, eds., *The Sum of our Parts*, p. 90.

27. Paul R. Spickard addresses the dilemma of multiracial individuals being defined by others, versus how they see themselves in his article "What Must I Be?: Asian Americans and the Question of Multiethnic Identity," in *Amerasia Journal*, Vol. 23, No. 1 (1997), pp. 44–45.

28. A similar response as an *Amerasian* or *Afroasian* is provided in H. Ricka Houston, "Between Two Cultures: A Testimony," in *Amerasia Journal*, Vol. 23, No. 1 (1997), pp. 149–154.

29. I must note that I am not using Mexipino as a means to privilege Mexican over Filipino identity. Phonetically the terms sounds better when combining both Mexican and Filipino to make one word to describe those that share in this multiethnic identity.

30. It can also be argued that Mexicans and Filipinos share not a single, but double colonial experience, because they were colonized by both the United States and Spain. As I gather more information on the common experiences of this double colonization, I will provide more insights as to how this affects their social, psychological, and economic positions in the U.S. today.

31. According to recent census information, Los Angeles has the largest Filipino population in the United States, followed by San Diego. Filipinos make up 4.3 percent of the total population in San Diego, which is about half of the total percentage for all Asians and Pacific Islanders. Mexicans make up 22.3 percent of the total population, ranking as the largest Latino ethnic group in San Diego. For more information see U.S. Census Bureau, Census 2000 Summary File 1, Matrices P3, P4, PCT4, PCT5, PCT8, and PCT11, 2001. <http://factfinder.census. gov/servlet/BasicFactsServlet> (22 April 2002).

32. As my research progresses, I will provide the necessary evidence to substantiate my claims that Mexicans and Filipinos, because of their similarities with Spanish surnames, religion, and physical appearance and color, were often recognized as an undifferentiated mass of brown people by outsiders, particularly Anglos, who treated them the same and saw no distinction between the two groups. As a result, they were put in similar circumstances and experienced similar discrimination, even though they did know within their groups the distinction between being Mexican and Filipino.

33. I must note that because this is a work-in-progress, I only had the opportunity to interview six Mexipinos for this particular paper. In addition to these six interviewees, I used some of my own experiences, as well as those of other Mexipinos that I spoke with in conversation, but did not have the opportunity to interview, to begin analyzing this particular multiethnic experience. My intentions are to continue interviewing Mexipinos in the attempts to compile a larger study to work with for my dissertation, thus providing me with a more diverse and complete analysis of what it means to be Mexipino in San Diego, California.

34. Root, *The Multiracial Experience*, pp. xiii–14.

35. See Paul R. Spickard, "The Illogic of American Racial Categories," in Maria P. P. Root, ed., *Racially Mixed People in America* (Newbury Park, California: Sage Publications, 1992), p. 21.

36. Christine C. Iijima Hall, "Best of Both Worlds: Body Image and Satisfaction of a Sample of Black-Japanese Biracial Individuals," *Amerasia Journal*, Vol. 23, No. 1 (1997), pp. 87–97.

37. Dale Soliven, interview by author, San Diego, Calif., 28 December 2001.

38. Marissa Mariscal, interview by author, Santa Barbara, Calif., 8 February 2002.

39. Rachael Ochoa-Tafoya, interview by author, Santa Barbara, Calif., 5 January 2002.

40. Dale Soliven, interview by author, San Diego, Calif., 28 December 2001.

41. Sophia Limjoco, telephone interview with author, 8 January 2002.

42. Dario Deguzman Villa, *The Bridge Generation: Sons and Daughters of Filipino Pioneers* (San Diego: Dario D. Villa, 1996), p. 2.

43. Sophia Limjoco, telephone interview with author, 8 January 2002.

44. Marissa Mariscal, interview by author, Santa Barbara, Calif., 8 February 2002.

45. Root, ed., *The Multiracial Experience*, pp. 8–9.

46. Teresa Williams-Leon addresses this issue of the "What are you?" question in her article "Race as Process: Reassessing the 'What are you?' Encounters of Biracial Individuals," in Maria P. P. Root, ed., *The Multiracial Experience: Racial Borders as the New Frontier* (Thousand Oaks, California: Sage Publications, 1996), pp. 203–209. See also Pearl Fuyo Gaskin, *What Are You?: Voices of Mixed-Race Young People* (New York: Henry, Holt and Company, 1999).

47. Marissa Mariscal, interview by author, Santa Barbara, Calif., 8 February 2002.

48. Jennifer Dixon, interview by author, San Diego, Calif., 29 December 2001; Marissa Mariscal, interview by author, Santa Barbara, Calif., 8 February 2002.; Dale Soliven, interview by author, San Diego, Calif., 28 December 2001; Susana Fernandez, interview by author, San Diego, Calif., 30 December 2001; Rachael Ochoa-Tafoya, interview by author, Santa Barbara, Calif., 5 January 2002; Sophia Limjoco, telephone interview with author, 8 January 2002.

49. Dale Soliven, interview by author, San Diego, Calif., 28 December 2001.

50. Root, ed., *The Multiracial Experience*, p. xxi.

51. Ibid., p. xxi.

52. Marissa Mariscal, interview by author, Santa Barbara, Calif., 8 February 2002.

53. Susana Fernandez, interview by author, San Diego, Calif., 30 December 2001.

54. Rachael Ochoa-Tafoya, interview by author, Santa Barbara, Calif., 5 January 2002; Jennifer Dixon, interview by author, San Diego, Calif., 29 December 2001; Sophia Limjoco, telephone interview with author, 8 January 2002.

55. Dale Soliven, interview by author, San Diego, Calif., 28 December 2002.

56. When I took a trip to the island of Oahu during the summer of 2001, I went to a Mexican restaurant and spoke to the waitress in Spanish. She was shocked that I spoke Spanish and told me that she didn't expect that from me because she thought I was a "local" Hawaiian. I interpreted her comment on my perceived identity based on my location, as well as the result of my physical appearance because I am multiethnic.

57. Williams-Leon and Nakashima, *The Sum of Our Parts*, p. 88.

58. Some of these experiences, which this interviewee recalls, were somewhat negative. This is why throughout my paper I mention the fact that "for the most part it was positive." Her experience was very different from the other interviews I conducted, and I suspect that her experience is not the only one like this. Nevertheless, I still contend that although there are these cases of negative experiences growing up multiethnic, this is not the case for the majority of Mexipinos, which I will suggest, says a lot about the ethnic relationship between Mexicans and Filipinos. Susana Fernandez, interview by author, San Diego, Calif., 30 December 2001.

59. Marissa Mariscal, interview by author, Santa Barbara, Calif., 8 February 2002.

60. Sophia Limjoco, telephone interview with author, 8 January 2002.

CHALLENGING THE HEGEMONY OF MULTICULTURALISM: THE MATTER OF THE MARGINALIZED MULTIETHNIC

JEFFREY A. S. MONIZ

UNIVERSITY OF CALIFORNIA, SANTA BARBARA

Abstract

Although multiculturalism, including cultural pluralism and multicultural education, has made progress in challenging White patriarchal supremacist hegemony, it, in itself, is also hegemonic. Multiculturalists, in their aspirations to assert diverse perspectives, often fail to consider those of mixed race and mixed ethnicity. Despite their efforts to reflect diversity, multiculturalists tend to utilize essentialized cultural categories that still marginalize many. This critique, from a multiethnic author engaged in multicultural education, aims to transform multiculturalism to be more inclusive. Reviewing other published critiques of multiculturalism and literature addressing multiracial/multiethnic issues provides the background for recommendations to extend the boundaries of diversity.

"It is a rare peasant who, once 'promoted' to overseer, does not become more of a tyrant towards his former comrades than the owner himself" (Freire, 2000, p. 46). Paulo Freire's words, in *Pedagogy of the Oppressed*, warned the oppressed that they must not perpetuate injustice in their quest for liberation. In the midst of their struggle, they need to avoid the tendency to become oppressors, or "sub-oppressors" themselves. Freire attributed this tendency to a duality that has established itself in the innermost being of the oppressed. He explained this duality as being, at one and the same time, themselves and the oppressors. They have internalized the consciousness of the oppressors (Freire, 2000).

This quotation from Freire is helpful in framing an enormous challenge faced by those who are concerned with issues of multiculturalism, cultural pluralism, and multicultural education. Postmodern analyses, focusing on the how conditions of power have shaped the identities of both the oppressed and the oppressors, alert us of the ways that many liberatory discourses actually reinscribe the very relations of power that they seek to challenge (Grant & Ladson-Billings, 1997). Multiculturalism, in its belief of strength and richness in human diversity and its goal of equality, equity, and social justice for all (Grant & Ladson-Billings, 1997) often fail to consider those of mixed race and mixed ethnicity, while vigorously asserting the respective agendas of racial and ethnic groups that are typically defined in monolithic, essentialized, and categorical terms. In the process of affirming the value of historically marginalized groups, most multiculturalists have inadvertently or purposefully ignored persons of mixed race and/or ethnicity. A postmodern critique would interrogate the systems of reasoning that created the categories used. What conditions of power construct the current state of multiculturalism? Although a thorough deconstruction of multiculturalism may be in order, the focal point of this particular critique, while building on some postmodern analyses, will eventually center, more specifically, on multiculturalism's marginalization of those who are racially and ethnically mixed.

At this point, a word about the terms used in this critique is in order. Because the terms employed in writing about multiculturalism and multiethnicity, two distinct constructs in the discussion of race and ethnicity, are somewhat idiosyncratic and often notoriously imprecise, nomenclature is always at issue. In the sections that follow I will define the constructs central to this discussion, according to sources that appear to be most clearly invested in the use of those terms. Thus, I will turn to scholars in multicultural education to define "multiculturalism," "cultural pluralism," and "multicultural education," and depend on constructionist sociologists concerned with the making of ethnicity and race as human creations, for a definition of "multiethnicity." Throughout the course of this narrative, I will refer to multiculturalism, cultural pluralism, and multicultural education, by simply using "multiculturalism," unless any distinctions or clarifications are necessary. I will also employ the use of the cover term "multiethnicity" and its derivative "multiethnic" to refer to issues of multiethnicity and multiraciality, unless a source that I'm citing does otherwise. The term "multiplicity" will also be used interchangeably with multiethnicity, although the use of multiplicity in other contexts often includes issues of gender, sexual orientation, physical disability, language, and socioeconomic status. Although it can be argued that issues of multiplicity that extend beyond race and ethnicity are often subject to the same kind of marginalization at the hands of multiculturalism, the present critique will only attempt to argue on behalf of multiethnics. This does not, in any way, devalue critiques from others marginalized by traditional multiculturalists. This would be hypocritical. Instead, I am bound by the limitations of space and can only hope that others will similarly take up their respective causes to argue for inclusion under the so-called diversity of multiculturalism.

It also needs to be made clear that this critique is not meant to be a blanket criticism of all of multiculturalism. There probably are multiculturalists who are concerned and may already be actively addressing the issue at hand. Most multiculturalists probably do not possess conscious intentions of marginalizing multiethnics. The hope of this critique is to raise the awareness of those involved in multiculturalism, especially in anticipation of the increasing numbers of multiethnic persons produced through an increase in interethnic unions. This increase has been and continues to be brought about by the heightened amount of inter-group contact caused by major migration movements stemming from destabilized and shifting economic and political situations. It has also come about due to the relaxing of anti-miscegenation attitudes and changes to laws brought about by the civil rights movement of the 1960s. These factors have created a situation that will produce a critical mass of multiethnic persons whose existence needs to be addressed, especially in American states like California, Texas, New York, and Florida. Maybe a logical place to start looking at ways that multiethnic persons have been acknowledged is the state whose population has been mixing in the relatively largest proportion for the longest amount of time. Looking at Hawai'i might provide a good preview of what we can expect as the rest of the nation becomes more multiethnic.

Multicultural and Multiethnic Hawai'i as an Example

According to the Census Bureau's 2000 count, more than 20 percent of Hawai'i residents reported ancestors of more than one race, giving the state a far higher percentage of multiracial inhabitants than the nation as a whole (Madden, 2001). Nationwide, only about 2.4 percent of residents indicated a multiracial heritage in the 2000 census. According to a brief released by the U.S. Census Bureau, Hawai'i, by far, has the highest percentage of multiracial inhabitants (Jones & Smith, 2001). Alaska and California follow by a big distance, percentage-wise, with 5.4 percent and 4.7 percent, respectively (Jones & Smith, 2001).

Over fifty years ago, nearly one-fourth of the children born in Hawai'i were of mixed racial ancestry (Fassler, 1998). The 1990 census indicated that 421,461 out of 1.1 million, over one-third of the total population, were considered "mixed" (Fassler, 1998). The most recent census also indicated that almost one-fourth of the state reported at least some Native Hawaiian ancestry, fifty-eight percent reported being at least part Asian, and about thirty-nine percent reported some white ancestry (Madden, 2001). In light of the old and recently released census data, it appears that the majority of Hawai'i residents born in the early part of this century will also fall into the multiracial category.

Diversity and mixing are not only a well-established aspect of life in Hawai'i, but it is true of other parts of the Pacific as well. Most Pacific Islanders have long recognized and embraced multiethnicity (Cornell & Hartmann, 1998). Multiethnicity was common in much of the Pacific before Europeans appeared (Cornell & Hartmann, 1998). When European explorers and settlers entered the scene, the scope of mixing grew tremendously. Colonial administrations and businessmen brought in Indian, Chinese, Japanese, more European, and an assortment of other workers. Historically, Hawai'i was a gathering spot for many of these peoples (Cornell & Hartmann, 1998), and as the part of the

United States in the middle of the Pacific, it continues to be a diverse gathering place.

The Growing Significance of Multiethnicity

Of course, mixed ancestry or multiethnicity is nothing new. It is an ancient phenomenon. The history of multiethnicity is as old as the history of interaction among distinct human peoples (Cornell & Hartmann, 1998). It's just that multiethnicity and multiraciality have seldom been acknowledged, must less celebrated, in other parts of the world. In Europe and the United States, mixed parentage was long viewed as a handicap. (This issue will be discussed further in a later section.) For much of American history, most people accepted the ethnic and racial categories that they were given for official purposes. That has changed in recent years. A growing number of Americans who possess more than one ethnic or racial background have become reluctant to choose one among them (Cornell & Hartmann, 1998). Hence, the 2000 census allowed respondents to self-select as many categories as they wanted.

In the United States interracial and interethnic marriage has been on the rise. Between 1970 and 1995, the number of interracial married couples more than tripled (Cornell & Hartmann, 1998). In *Postethnic America*, the historian David Hollinger painted a picture of contemporary America prior to the 2000 census. He described an ethno-racial pentagon in which five ethno-racial blocs (Euro-American or White, Asian American, African American, Hispanic or Latino, and Indigenous Peoples or Native American) live side by side, ignoring each other and ignoring the poor and powerless in their midst (Hollinger, 1995). As Hollinger predicted, the logic of mixed race has destroyed the structure of America's ethno-racial pentagon. This has been acknowledged with the recent changes to our census but is more evident in the continuously and exponentially growing number of multiethnic people.

In 1992, the U.S. Bureau of the Census reported that the number of biracial babies was increasing at a faster rate than the number of monoracial babies (Root, 1996). The National Center for Health Statistics noted that the number of monoracial babies has grown at a rate of 15 percent since the early 1970s, while the number of multiracial babies has increased more than 260 percent (Root, 1996). Maria Root, a leading researcher of multiraciality, pointed out the following:

> Although multiracial births represent a small portion of babies born in the United States (3.4 percent in 1989, when race was recorded for both parents), this translates into over 100,000 births per year since at least 1989. More than a million first-generation biracial individuals have been born in this country since then. This figure will rapidly increase according to demographic projection, even if interracial marriage rates remain constant (Alonso & Waters, 1993, quoted in Root, 1996b, p. xv).

Root also described how the trends are similar across racial groups by reporting U.S. Census Bureau data published in 1992. The bureau reported that while the number of monoracial Black babies has grown 27 percent and the number of monoracial White babies 15 percent, the number of Black/White biracial babies has grown almost 500 percent (Root, 1996). According to the Census Bureau, there were 39 percent more Japanese/White births than monoracial Japanese American births in 1990 (Root, 1996). Among Native Americans, there were 40 percent more racially mixed babies than babies born to two parents who identify as American Indian. Root also noted that this trend was also present for other Asian American and Pacific Islander groups (Root, 1996).

Interracial marriage and mutiraciality are significantly altering the American demographic landscape. These changes in our nation's makeup will soon have a greater impact on racially and ethnically conscious remedies for social and political change. Multiculturalism in the 21st century will have to adapt to address these changes. The current state of multiculturalism barely recognizes and considers the issues of the multiethnic for a number of reasons. In order to interrogate those reasons, it is necessary to delve deeper into the emergence of multiculturalism and review some of its current critiques. The best way to effect any worthwhile change in multiculturalism is to begin by recognizing its strengths and to make visible its shortcomings. Until this is done, multiculturalism will hypocritically be as hegemonic as the White supremacy that it aims to replace.

Multiculturalism Defined and Critiqued

The terms "multiculturalism" and "multicultural education" have been appropriated and co-opted so often, by so many, that some in the field of Multicultural Education have recommended a moratorium of the use of those terms (Ladson-Billings, 2000). Because multiculturalism can mean different things to different people, in different contexts, the definitions of "multiculturalism," "cultural pluralism," and "multicultural education" presented here have been drawn from the source that I aim to critique, which is also the group in which I claim membership. These definitions, which are shortened and paraphrased for the sake of brevity, come from the *Dictionary of Multicultural Education* edited by Carl A. Grant and Gloria Ladson-Billings (1997).

Harold Chu, drawing from Cherry McGee Banks and James Banks, wrote:

> Multiculturalism is a philosophical position and movement that assumes that the gender, ethnic, racial, and cultural diversity of a pluralistic society should be reflected in all of its institutionalized structures but especially in educational institutions, including the staff, norms and values, curriculum, and student body (Banks & Banks, 1993, quoted by Chu in Grant & Ladson-Billings, 1997, p. 182).

Chu emphasized that defining "multiculturalism" only by the categories of race and ethnicity would be misleading. "Instead, cultural identity is based on traits and values learned as part of our ethnic origin, religion, gender, age, socioeconomic level, primary language, geographical region, place of residence and disabilities or exceptional conditions" (Chu in Grant & Ladson-Billings, 1997, pp. 182–83). It is important to note that Chu does recognize multiplicity in his dictionary entry. He mentioned that individuals with competencies in several microcultures develop a fuller appreciation of the range of cultural competencies available to all individuals. He added that those who have competencies in two or more different cultures are bicultural or multicultural and are often multilingual as well. Chu concluded his definition by stating that one's identity is more flexible, autonomous, and stable to the degree that one recognizes one's self as a member of various different subcommunities, simultaneously (in Grant & Ladson-Billings, 1997).

At first glance, it appears that this definition addresses racial and ethnic multiplicity of individuals, especially since Chu explicitly emphasized the simultaneous membership of various communities. One could wonder, though, if a cultural category for multiethnicity has been constructed. If it has, it would certainly fall under the auspices of multiculturalism as defined by Chu. Even if a space has been or is currently being constructed for multiethnicity, how has it been received or acknowledged? In any case, although inclusion in a sanctioned definition is a start, it does not accurately reflect the reality in practice, at least in the case of multiethnicity. In practice, monocultural categories reign supreme, and each different culture being referred to is ordinarily viewed as monolithic and usually in an essentialized fashion. (This is also a critique of ethnicity, which I will describe later in this section.)

"Cultural pluralism" was defined by Donna Gollnick in the dictionary. Citing Green, she wrote:

> Cultural pluralism implies cultural diversity, equality among groups, and a commitment to the value of diversity in society. The supporting values include belief in the freedom of association, belief that there is no single best way of life, belief that society must allow for many competing ways of life, and acknowledgement that different ways of life can interact and compete without changing each other (Green, 1966, cited by Gollnick in Grant & Ladson-Billings, 1997, p. 63).

The part of the definition that I found most valuable states that no single group rules over or exploits another. "It [cultural pluralism] extols the value of *e pluribus unum* in which many groups exist while supporting and developing a 'cohesive society whose culture is enriched by sharing widely divergent ethnic experiences'" (Pai, 1990, p. 97, quoted in Grant & Ladson-Billings, 1997, p. 64). This part of the definition is what makes cultural pluralism vulnerable to this critique. The intent expressed in this definition is often not reflected in the practices of multiculturalists.

Another problematic part of the definition of "cultural pluralism" is the part that directly concerns education. It reads:

> Cultural pluralism requires that the diversity of students and communities be understood, valued, and integrated in

all aspects of the educational process. The curriculum must reflect the diversity of the nation and the world; it cannot be centered in a single culture. Students must see themselves in the pages of their textbooks. Representations used by teachers to help students learn must be drawn from students' own cultural backgrounds (Grant & Ladson-Billings, 1997, p. 65).

This requirement imposed by cultural pluralism makes more sense if cultures are viewed as monolithic. What happens when we decide to recognize multiethnic children? How can we begin to attempt to represent every possible racial and ethnic mix in our diverse school population? If an attempt is made to represent multiplicity, which mixes will be privileged when selecting representatives? Granted, multiracial and multiethnic children are often featured as models in school texts and mainstream media, although probably for the simple reasons that they qualify as representatives of underrepresented groups while appearing more palatable, or tantalizingly exotic, to mainstream (White) tastes. Cultural pluralism's representation requirement initially appeared to be a noble one, but after further analysis, the requirement takes us back to the question of hegemony. When some images of the dominant culture are intentionally replaced by images representative of various historically underrepresented monocultures, who, ultimately, still gets left out?

The definition of "multicultural education" was provided by the dictionary's editors, Carl Grant and Gloria Ladson-Billings. They made it clear in their definition that multicultural education is a total process that cannot be truncated, emphasizing that all the components of its definition must be in place for multicultural education to be genuine and viable (Grant & Ladson-Billings, 1997). Due to this emphatic pronouncement, I am compelled to present most of the actual definition, almost in its entirety. For the sake of brevity, portions of the definition not directly mentioning the components were omitted:

> Multicultural education is a philosophical concept and an educational process ... It prepares all students to work actively toward structural equality in the organizations and institutions of the United States. It helps students to develop accurate self-concepts and accurate conceptions of

others, to discover who they are, particularly in terms of their multiple group memberships. Multicultural education does this by providing knowledge about the history, culture, and contributions of the diverse groups that have shaped the history, politics, and culture of the United States.

Multicultural education acknowledges and affirms the belief that the strength and richness of the United States is in its human diversity. It demands a school staff that is multiracial, multiculturally literate, including some staff members who are fluent in more that [sic] one language. It demands a teaching staff that reflects gender and race diversity across subject matter areas. It demands a curriculum that organizes concepts and content around the contributions, perspectives, and experiences of all the groups that are a part of U.S. society. It confronts current social issues involving race, socioeconomic status (SES), gender, sexuality, and disability. It accomplishes this by providing instruction in a social-cultural context that students understand and are familiar with, and builds upon students' learning styles. It teaches critical thinking skills, as well as democratic decision making, social action, and empowerment skills (Grant & Ladson-Billings, 1997, pp. xxvi-xxvii).

They conclude their definition by reiterating multicultural education's goal of equality, equity, and social justice for all.

This definition given by Grant and Ladson-Billings is consistent with my notion of an education that is equal, equitable, and socially just. Unfortunately, like the prior definitions of "multiculturalism" and "cultural pluralism," this definition represents the ideal and not what is actually being reflected in practice. It is also unfortunate that approaches with less desirable intentions, from my standpoint, have misappropriated the multicultural name, resulting in mistaken identity. On one hand, these poseur brands of multiculturalism and multicultural education are to blame for the amount of criticism that multiculturalism receives. On the other hand, the lines separating different brands of multiculturalism are often blurred, and a great deal of borrowing, appropriating, and misappropriating, even among those who consider themselves true multiculturalists, result in much deserved criticism.

For example, in his critique of multicultural education in

Toronto, Canada, Aminur Rahim (1990) described the prevalent approach to multiculturalism endorsed by the School Board. In this model, referred to as "the education of the culturally different," or "benevolent multiculturalism," all students, including those who are culturally different from the dominant ethnic group in society, should be given equal opportunity for learning. This is, of course, assuming that providing them with the same school facilities such as books and teachers will increase their abilities to pursue their courses of study and increase their chances of succeeding in an academic career (Rahim, 1990). Forgotten in all this is that the so-called equal opportunity, based on norms drawn from the dominant group, actually still disadvantages those who are different. At best, this model of multiculturalism is paternalistic. This "false generosity" on the part of the oppressors has helped to nourish the inequalities that continue to thrive (Freire, 2000).

A different critique, though also concerning a level of deception, was presented by E. San Juan, Jr. in his call to revitalize the critical and emancipatory thrust of Ethnic Studies, the immediate forebear of multiculturalism. He cautioned that ethnicity cannot be understood apart from history, the workings of the state, and the contingencies of political economy (San Juan, 1995). He warned against "ethnicism," which is the absolutizing or mystification of ethnicity, because it occludes racism and delegitimizes resistance to it (San Juan, 1995).

Along the lines of absolutizing ethnicity and critiquing models of multiculturalism, Marco Martiniello called attention to a shortcoming of many approaches to multiculturalism—the trap of essentializing cultures and identities (Martiniello, 1998). If one believes that an individual belongs to one culture only and displays only one ethno-national identity, he is actually adopting a highly debatable essentialist and primordial view of culture and identity (Martiniello, 1998).

W. M. Verhoeven, in a critique of pure ethnicity, discussed an essentialist notion of ethnic identity by contrasting Indian writers. One Indian writer, whom I will refer to here as the critic, chastised another for slavishly and uncritically adopting and internalizing the imperialists' esthetics and ideology of the colonial (British) oppressor, thus denying his own ethnic roots and stifling the "voice of otherness" in himself (Verhoeven, 1996). In

contrast, the critic ranked another Indian writer as more significant and ideologically relevant because he wrote within the
cultural tradition of his once-colonized fatherland (Verhoeven,
1996). This is a prime example of a value judgement, on the part
of the critic, based on her essentialist ideal of pure ethnicity.
Martha Nussbaum provided an excellent point in this regard:
"Cultures are not monolithic or static. Cultures contain many
strands; they contain conflict and rebellion; they evolve over time
and incorporate new ideas, sometimes from other cultures"
(Nussbaum, 1997, p. 117).

The issue of pure ethnicity challenges competing notions
from within the same ethnic group. Critiques of ethnicity and
multiculturalism also point out the competitive nature of disputes
beyond the boundaries of monolithically conceived essentialized
ethnic groups, especially when multiethnic persons disrupt the
equilibrium. For some, the idea of diversity becoming too diversi-
fied threatens essentialist notions of identity. Hollinger (1995)
pointed out the sheer hypocrisy of this notion when he described
how mixed-race Americans, demanding recognition, complicated
the argument over what kinds of sameness and what kinds of difference matter. He portrayed the defenders of the ethno-racial
pentagon as saying, "We don't want that kind of diversity because
it undermines the sameness necessary for identity." Hollinger
cleverly argued that this attitude is really no different from the
concerns voiced by Arthur M. Schlesinger, Jr., and others on
behalf of America, in Schlesinger's best-selling 1992 book, *The
Disuniting of America* (Hollinger, 1995). Voices of conservative
ethno-racial pentagon defenders ironically play the role of
Schlesinger to the mixed-race radical disuniters (Hollinger, 1995).

Henry Giroux also described this phenomenon in identity
politics. He wrote:

> While identity politics was central to challenging the cul-
> tural homogeneity of the 1950s ... [i]dentity politics en-
> abled many formerly silenced and displaced groups to
> emerge from the margins of power and dominant culture
> to reassert and reclaim suppressed identities and ex-
> periences; but in doing so, they often substituted one mas-
> ter narrative for another, invoked a politics of separatism,
> and suppressed differences within their own "liberatory"
> narratives (Giroux, 1994, p. 31).

Indeed, according to Hollinger and Giroux, Freire's observations appear to be accurate. "Almost always, during the initial stage of the struggle, the oppressed, instead of striving for liberation, tend themselves to become oppressors, or 'sub-oppressors'" (Freire, 2000, p. 45). Identity politics and the new cultural racism currently marginalize persons of mixed race and ethnicity. Moving from the margins to the center or pushing the borders further out is one of many challenges faced by the marginalized multiethnic. In order to understand the multiethnic's relationship to multiculturalism, a better grasp of the range of issues is in order. The next section contains a brief review of some of these multiethnic issues that are most relevant to multiculturalism.

Multiracial and Multiethnic Issues

Multiculturalism is different from multiethnicity (Cornell & Hartmann, 1998). Discussions of multiculturalism are about the presence and proper placement of different identities and groups in a single society. Multiethnicity, in contrast, refers to the mixing of ethnic and racial identities and ancestries in single persons (Cornell & Hartmann, 1998). "Multiethnicity is a product of human movement and mixing, and although the mixing of human peoples is very old indeed, the magnitude of movement among human populations has grown enormously in recent centuries" (Cornell & Hartmann, 1998). In this statement, Cornell and Hartmann acknowledged the human participation in the intermixing of groups since time immemorial, but also alluded to the enormous increase that has resulted in the current state of marked multiplicity.

A number of common psychological, social, and political issues accompany the critical mass of multiethnic persons. For example, there has been a common misconception, perpetuated by social science in the 20th century, that viewed persons of mixed parentage as psychologically disturbed and socially disruptive (Cornell & Hartmann, 1998). Interracial offspring have often been portrayed as tortured souls in popular films and literature (e.g., the popular depiction of the tragic mulatto) (Spickard, 1989). Ronald Johnson's study of the offspring of cross-race and cross-ethnic marriages in Hawai'i refuted this popular presumption. Persons of mixed parentage do not necessarily have to fulfill the stereotype. He found that the offspring of cross-group marriages showed no signs of psychological disturbances (Johnson, 1992). In fact, they performed significantly better than the offspring of within-group marriages on tests of cognitive ability and were not more at risk for problem drinking (Johnson, 1992).

One cannot deny that feelings of difference and discrepancy among multiethnics, as they seek understanding from others as a way of understanding themselves, probably do contribute to psychological problems in many, especially in a society that regularly relegates them to the margins. To many Americans, the multiethnic represents the perpetual *other*. There is a strong possibility that the results reported for the Hawai'i study may only be true for Hawai'i or societies like Hawai'i, where personal attributes are often regarded as more important than race in mate selection (Johnson, 1992). In Hawai'i society, multiplicity appears less likely to be associated with psychological problems than the rest of the United States.

For most in the other forty-nine states, multiethnic people disconcertingly blur the boundaries between the "us" and "them." "Jean Paul Sartre suggested that people define self in terms of the subjective experience of the other" (cited in Root, 1996a, p. 9). Multiracial people, in this case, usually do not fit neatly into the observer's notion of reality (Root, 1996). The "normal" citizen possesses a limited understanding of the mixed person's place in society (Root, 1996). Root described this understanding as "images abound of slave masters raping black women, U.S. military men carrying on sexually illicit relationships with Asian women during wars, and rebels and curiosity seekers having casual affairs" (Root, 1996a, p. 7). The multiethnic's existence challenges the rigidity of ethnic and racial lines that are a prerequisite for maintaining the delusion that race is a scientific fact (Root, 1996). Often, this rigidity results in a tyranny that require mixed persons to exaggerate caricatures of ethnic and racial stereotypes in order to justify their legitimacy (Root, 1996). Multiethnic people also are faced with choosing identities different than what others wish to impose on them. They often grapple with the identities projected onto them not only by strangers, but also by parents and siblings. Persons of mixed background are often also confused with choices to identify differently depending on different situations (Root, 1996).

The call to justify one's legitimacy is a major effect of the essentialized way that culture, race, and ethnicity are constructed. An example of this was presented in Rebecca Chiyoko King's study of mixed-race Japanese Americans who participated in the Cherry Blossom Queen Pageant (King, 1997). The pageant, conducted by members of San Francisco's Japanese American community, annually selects the woman who best symbolizes "Japanese-ness" and represents Japanese Americans. King described how a mixed-race candidate saw herself as Japanese, but was denied that identification by other monoracial Japanese (King, 1997). Mixed-race candidates expressed that other people thought that the queen should be 100 percent Japanese and that full-bloodedness is related to knowledge of culture (King, 1997). This resulted in mixed-race candidates feeling additional pressure to prove their Japanese-ness (King, 1997).

This example clearly illustrated how the manner in which ethnicity, race, and culture are constructed is problematic. The way that people are categorized places limitations on the very existence of multiethnic and multiracial individuals. The next section will explore the possibilities and limits of transforming multiculturalism and, more specifically, multicultural education, in order to respond to the challenge at hand.

Multicultural Education and the Transformation of Multiculturalism

Although multicultural education has worked to address the challenges that our schools face in the education of diverse populations, current discourses about race and ethnicity within schools can be characterized by a general fixation on cultural differences tied to essentialist constructions of identity (Glass & Wallace, 1996). An assumption exists that existing cultural or racial manifestations are naturally given, unchanging, and all-defining (Glass & Wallace, 1996). "In order to challenge racism, educators must move away from an infatuation with fixed racial identities and toward a thoughtful reconsideration of racism as a 'total social phenomenon' that obscures the ideological foundations of identity" (Balibar, 1991, quoted in Glass & Wallace,

1996, p. 353). Responding to this challenge requires an evalua-
tion of the way crosscultural and multicultural education courses
are taught.

A major and often unstated focus of crosscultural and multicultural education courses is to educate and enlighten Euro-
Americans about the impact of race, ethnicity, and culture
(Williams et al., 1996). Although these courses are well-inten-
tioned, they often have an underlying paternalistic view about
people of color (Williams et al., 1996). Williams, Nakashima,
Kich, and Daniel wrote about these courses: "They legitimize the
separation and inequality across racial and ethnic groups; they
foster learning about *other* peoples' cultures; and they assume,
if not perpetuate, the notion of race with distinct borders"
(Williams et al., 1996, p. 361). They also aptly pointed out the
fact that interracial relationships are often missing, and that subsequently multiraciality is erased out of textual and experiential
existence (Williams et al., 1996).

Francis Wardle, in an essay on multicultural education,
provided a statement that serves to recount and summarize some
of the issues presented in this critique. He wrote:

> The conventional model for multicultural education does
> not allow us to support the history, identity, and healthy
> development of biracial children. By dividing our country's
> population into five traditional groups, we always force
> biracial children to reject a significant part of their heritage.
> Furthermore, most multicultural publications create the
> false dichotomy of white people in one camp and people of
> color in the other. Again, this artificial battlefield places the
> biracial child in a position of conflicting loyalties and psy-
> chological stress (Bowles, 1993 and Wardle, 1992, quoted
> in Wardle, 1996, pp. 382–83).

Wardle also reiterated the major point made earlier that the traditional model is incorrect and misleading when teaching our students that American society is made up of five distinctly
different, unified, homogenous groups (Wardle, 1996). He made
a suggestion, which I wholeheartedly agree with, to change the
way that we look at people in this country. Instead of placing
people in sociopolitical groups, we must view each person as an
individual affected by a variety of influences (Wardle, 1996).
These influences include, but are not limited to, race, ethnicity,

and family (Wardle, 1996). Although Wardle is concerned with influences rather than the notion of multiple group membership, his ideas concerning multicultural education sound somewhat similar to Chu's definition of multiculturalism. In both cases, there is a definite regard for individuality and flexibility. Wardle concluded, "Thus a true multicultural curriculum must respond to, reflect, and support the unique set of experiences every child brings to our programs" (Wardle, 1994, quoted in Wardle, 1996, p. 383).

Conclusion

The challenge posed to multiculturalism by the marginalized multiethnic cannot be left unanswered, nor should the marginalized accept their status. Those who are marginalized should seek to take an active role in constructing their identities for themselves. Peter McLaren wrote, "Educators would do well to consider Gloria Anzaldua's (1987) project of creating *mestizaje* theories that create new categories of identity for those left out or pushed out of existing ones" (McLaren, 1994, p. 218). McLaren, citing Houston Baker (1985, p. 388), also reminded us that we must move beyond pedagogies of protest, which only reinforces the dualism of self and other, reinstates the basis of dominant racist evaluations, and preserves the " 'always already' arrangements of White patriarchal hegemony" (McLaren, 1994, p. 218). Another option could be to abandon identity grouping. Instead of reifying cultural traits, we could show how allegedly fixed and static attributes change under the pressure of circumstances and the transformative force of people's actions (San Juan, 1995). Whatever the case, one thing is for sure, a transformation must take place.

In pondering the transformation being called for, I turned to Cornell West's reassessment of the critical legal studies movement. He wrote, "To see solely the ways in which dominant versions of liberalism domesticate and dilute such oppositonal activities is to view liberalism in too monolithic and homogenous a manner" (West, 1993, p. 201). His words reminded me, that in my critique of multiculturalism, I must remember that not all multiculturalists have assumed the role of oppressor. West added, "...leftist oppositional thought and practice should build on the best of liberalism, yet transform liberalism in a more democratic and egalitarian manner" (West, 1993, p. 203). These words inspired the following charge that grew from this critique: In order to build a multiculturalism that is more inclusive and values multiethnicity, we must build on the best of multiculturalism and multicultural education, yet transform multiculturalism and multicultural education in a more democratic and egalitarian manner.

The critical mass of acknowledged mixed people presents a challenge to multiculturalism. In order to transcend divisions, we must be able to look across these divisions with respect (Nussbaum, 1997, p. 67). To achieve this respect, we need to pursue a fuller humanity. "The struggle to become more fully human has already begun in the authentic struggle to transform the situation" (Freire, 2000, p. 47).

My hunch and hope is that one significant result of this process is that multiculturalism and multicultural education will become more conscious of issues of multiethnicity and multiraciality. If multiculturalism continues to marginalize mixed people, those who call themselves multiculturalists will be guilty of the same kind of discrimination and hypocrisy usually attributed to the White patriarchal hegemony that we initially sought to subvert.

References

Cornell, S. E., & Hartmann, D. (1998). *Ethnicity and race: Making identities in a changing world*. Thousand Oaks, CA: Pine Forge Press.

Fassler, C. R. (1998). *Rainbow kids: Hawaii's gift to America*. Honolulu: White Tiger Press.

Freire, P. (2000). *Pedagogy of the oppressed*. New York : Continuum.

Giroux, H. A. (1994). Living dangerously: Identity politics and the new cultural racism. In H. A. Giroux & P. McLaren (Eds.), *Between borders: Pedagogy and the politics of cultural studies* (pp. 29–55). New York; London: Routledge.

Glass, R. D., & Wallace, K. R. (1996). Challenging race and racism: A framework for educators. In M. P. P. Root (Ed.), *The multiracial experience: Racial borders as the new frontier* (pp. 341–58). London [Eng]; Thousand Oaks, CA: Sage.

Grant, C. A., & Ladson-Billings, G. (1997). *Dictionary of multicultural education*. Phoenix, AZ: Oryx Press.

Hollinger, D. A. (1995). *Postethnic America: Beyond multiculturalism.* New York: BasicBooks.

Johnson, R. C. (1992). Offspring of cross-race and cross-ethnic marriages in Hawaii. In M. P. P. Root (Ed.), *Racially mixed people in America* (pp. 239–49). Newbury Park, CA: Sage Publications.

Jones, N. A. & Smith, A. S. (2001). The two or more races population: 2000. U.S. Census Bureau Brief, no. C2KBR/01-6, November 2001.

King, R. C. (1997). Multiraciality reigns supreme?: Mixed-Race Japanese Americans and the Cherry Blossom Queen Pageant. *Amerasia Journal,* 23(1), 113-128.

Ladson-Billings, G. (Speaker). (2000, April). *Multicultural education in the 21st century: Multiple perspectives on its past, present, and future.* Symposium presented at the annual meeting of the American Educational Research Association, New Orleans, LA. (Cassette Recording No. 200424-12.20) La Crescenta, CA: Audio Archives International, Inc. (2000).

Madden, M. (2001, March 20). Hawai'i: A racial rainbow. *The Honolulu Advertiser.*

Martiniello, M. (1998). Wieviorka's view on multiculturalism: A critique. (comment on article by Michel Wieviorka in this issue, p. 881) (Special Issue: Rethinking Ethnic and Racial Studies). *Ethnic and Racial Studies,* 21(5), 911 (916 pages).

McLaren, P. (1994). Multiculturalism and the post-modern critique: Toward a pedagogy of resistance and transformation. In H. A. Giroux & P. McLaren (Eds.), *Between borders: Pedagogy and the politics of cultural studies* (pp. 192–222). New York; London: Routledge.

Nussbaum, M. C. (1997). *Cultivating humanity: A classical defense of reform in liberal education.* Cambridge, MA: Harvard University Press.

Rahim, A. (1990). Multiculturalism or ethnic hegemony: A critique of multicultural education in Toronto. *Journal of Ethnic Studies,* 18(3), 29 (18 pages).

Root, M. P. P. (1996a). A bill of rights for racially mixed people. In M. P. P. Root (Ed.), *The multiracial experience: Racial borders as the new frontier* (pp. 3–14). London; Thousand Oaks, CA: Sage.

Root, M. P. P. (1996b). The multiracial experience: Racial borders as a significant frontier in race relations. In M. P. P. Root (Ed.), *The multiracial experience: Racial borders as the new frontier* (pp. xii–xxviii). London; Thousand Oaks, CA: Sage.

San Juan, E., Jr. (1995). Beyond ethnicity: Toward a critique of the hegemonic discipline. *Explorations in Ethnic Studies,* 18(2), 131 (114 pages).

Spickard, P. R. (1989). *Mixed blood: Intermarriage and ethnic identity in twentieth-century America.* Madison, WI: University of Wisconsin Press.

Verhoeven, W. M. (1996). How hyphenated can you get?: A critique of pure ethnicity. (Idols of Otherness: The Rhetoric and Reality of Multiculturalism). *Mosaic* (Winnipeg), 29(3), 97 (20 pages).

Wardle, F. (1996). Multicultural education. In M. P. P. Root (Ed.), *The multiracial experience: Racial borders as the new frontier* (pp. 380–94). London; Thousand Oaks, CA: Sage.

West, C. (1993). *Keeping faith: Philosophy and race in America.* New York: Routledge.

Williams, T. K., Nakashima, C. L., Kich, G. K., & Daniel, G. R. (1996). Being different together in the university classroom: Multiracial identity as transgressive education. In M. P. P. Root (Ed.), *The multiracial experience: Racial borders as the new frontier* (pp. 359–79). London; Thousand Oaks, CA: Sage.

BEYOND DISOBEDIENCE

NICOLE M. WILLIAMS

UNIVERSITY OF CALIFORNIA, SANTA BARBARA

Abstract

Research has shown that students with oppositional identity must employ "border-crossing strategies" in order to pursue academic success. These strategies allow the student to succeed in school without jeopardizing his or her social status. Border-crossing strategies have only been found to be used by individuals; furthermore, these individuals generally hide their efforts to do well in school from their peers. An examination of classroom discourse in a California continuation school, however, shows how a class of students used code-switching during class time as a border crossing strategy.

When I began my research, I intended to study the effect that a multicultural social studies curriculum was having on students in a junior high continuation school. As I observed the class, I noticed that the students spent very little time engaged with the content of the curriculum and much more time disrupting the teacher's efforts to teach. Consequently, I decided to try and understand the academic and behavioral choices the students were making. It was interesting to me that the students openly resisted participating in class events despite their consistent attendance and clearly expressed desire to return to a mainstream campus. The focus of this study became an attempt to understand how and why the students were negotiating that contradictory behavior.

Data Set

The site from which the data for this analysis was collected is part of the Continuation system on the central coast of California. When junior and senior high school students are not earning enough academic credit to graduate on time, they are referred to a continuation school. Each continuation site consists of two portable classrooms located somewhere on the fringes of a mainstream school campus. Sidelines School, where I collected my data, exists in the back of a very affluent junior high school campus. The majority of the students at the mainstream junior high are white. The Sidelines School consists of the two portables enclosed by a chain-linked fence. Of approximately 30 students, 26 were Latino, including Chicanos, Mexican immigrants, students of Mexican descent, and Guatemalans; two were African American, one was European American and one was Chumash Native American. The grade levels of the students in the class of study ranged from seventh to ninth.

The teacher in the classroom was a non-Spanish speaking, Yugoslav, New Yorker, who had been teaching for at least eighteen years. He was teaching social studies, and his particular goal was to teach history from a relevant and multicultural perspective. Many of his lessons focused on the Latino, Native American, and African-American perspectives of North American history.

The Data Set consists of 8 student interviews of one-half to two-and-a-half hours in length and one three-hour teacher interview. All of the interviews were transcribed. There is a total of 22.5 hours of participant observation recorded on videotapes and fieldnotes. I visited the class at least once per week for four months. A running record (Green & Meyer, 1991) of shifts in activity within events was created for each class visited that incorporated the information from the fieldnotes and videotapes.

Oppositional Identity and Sub-Culture

I began my theoretical analysis of the data with John Ogbu's (1985; 1992; 1995; 1998) work on oppositional identity and involuntary minorities. According to Ogbu minority groups that become members of a country's population involuntarily, through some form of domination like slavery, develop a cultural frame of reference in opposition to the mainstream culture. This means that the minority group members deem certain behaviors as more appropriate for members of the mainstream culture and other behaviors as more appropriate for the minority group members. This theory is demonstrated, for example, when an African-American tells another African-American person to stop "acting white."

Fordham and others like Patthey-Chavez (Fordham, 1988; 1999; Fordham & Ogbu, 1986; Mehan, Hubbard, & Villanueava, 1994; Patthey-Chavez, 1993) have used Ogbu's theories to gain understanding of the overwhelming resistance of various U.S. minorities to school activities. Their research shows that the school failure of involuntary minorities is a result of deliberate acts of resistance integrally tied to the oppositional frame of reference, which Ogbu claims is inherent in involuntary minority cultures. Consequently, it is argued that for involuntary minorities, doing school activities is perceived as "acting white." According to Fordham and others (Fordham, 1988; 1999; Fordham & Ogbu, 1986; Mehan, Hubbard, and Villanueava, 1994; Patthey-Chavez, 1993), the issue of non-participation in school for minority students then is not an issue of ability or motivation, as practitioners often believe. The crux of the problem for involuntary minorities resides in the students' need to negotiate cultural group allegiances.

I attempted to understand the resistance of the students in the Sidelines classroom in light of Ogbu's theories. I considered Matute-Bianchi's (1986) description of what it means to be a Chicano.

> It means sitting in the back in a class of "gabachos" and not participating; it means not carrying books to class or doing your homework; ... it means doing the minimum to get by. In short, it means not participating in school in ways that will promote academic success and achievement... They must choose between doing well in school or being a Chicano (p. 240).

Many of the cultural norms that correspond to the oppositional frame of reference were prevalent in the Sidelines data. My observations suggested that the students were a close knit social group. This observation was confirmed when asked in the interviews if the student population had different cliques, or if one group of students was more popular than another, or if the student population was divided into categories in any way. The resounding response was: "No, we all get along pretty good, we are all friends." Likewise, student behavior was often governed by group norms. In an interview with one student, he revealed that the majority of student efforts to disrupt that appeared to be individual were actually planned and required by the students to act as a group.

> But yea it was like a set up like, "Ehh let's get the teacher mad, or eh let's not listen to [the teacher], or like even in Spanish sometimes like they would say like, "Oh naw, naw, don't tell her who did it" and so like they'd be, "No no no le diga" (Sidelines student).

This point is further illustrated by looking at an example of implicit group norms made explicit in a conversation that occurred in the Sidelines classroom. The teacher was particularly frustrated because every time he tried to speak to the class, the students would start talking. In the following excerpt a new and young seventh grade student notices the trend but does not understand it. At the end of the excerpt, an older (meaning in age and time in the class) student explains the problem.

> Seventh grader: [Teacher], how come when, you know, when you say "quiet" right and people stay quiet and [inaudible] then you start talking and then people start talking again?
>
> Teacher: Yes, so what?
>
> Seventh grader: Yea.
>
> Teacher: Why? That's my question, I know as soon as I start talking you start talking so I don't know [inaudible] perhaps you don't want to hear what I have to say and [inaudible]
>
> Eighth grader: We *gotta* comment to try to be funny.

Another similarity between the Chicanos described in Matute-Bianchi's (1986) article and the Sidelines students was that many students made deliberate efforts to mask their academic ability, in addition to calling people who participated in class activities "nerds" and "teacher's pet." In a description of his classmate one student says:

> But he does his work, he's pretty smart, but he just like stays out like instead of doing his work when he can do it you know he goes and talks to people you know, tries to bug [the teacher] sometimes. I guess he, he gets tired after awhile. Like me too I can be a good student but I get tired of being

good, you get no comments for being good, you get more.... (Sidelines student).

Despite the fact that the *culture of opposition* very clearly existed in this class, the problem that I found in applying Ogbu's theory to my own data was that the group of students were ethnically and racially mixed as well as being both involuntary and voluntary minorities.

Much of the research on oppositional identity, as it applies to students in schools, has been conducted in what was depicted as ethnically and racially homogenous populations (Fordham, 1999; Mehan et al., 1994), and thus, like Ogbu's theory, does not account for inter-group variation. When similar studies are conducted considering inter-group variation, it is shown that the oppositional frame of reference actually exists amongst sub-groups of the larger racial or ethnic categorization. Matute-Bianchi's (1986) research shows that within the Mexican-American ethnic group there are several sub-groups, and it is the Chicano and Cholo sub-groups whose cultural norms include an oppositional frame of reference toward school.

When the oppositional frame of reference theory is applied in terms of sub-cultural groups in schools, as opposed to entire ethnic groups, it can be expanded beyond the bounds of race and ethnicity. The factor that makes oppositional sub-cultures oppositional is marginalization. While ethnic group membership is often a very salient aspect of commonality amongst the members of an oppositional sub-culture, it is perceived marginalization that is the most salient boundary marker for member inclusion. Brake (1985) defines sub-cultures as:

> Meaning systems, modes of expression or life styles developed by groups in subordinate structural positions in response to dominant meaning systems, and which reflect their attempt to solve structural contradictions arising from the wider societal context (p. 8).

Another factor that is integrally tied to ethnicity and is salient for sub-culture boundary definition is language. Language is one way in which the students define and or create distance between other groups and themselves. In her study of an all-white school in Detroit, Eckert (1989) found the existence of the oppositional frame of reference amongst many of the white working class students in the school. The following excerpt is her description of the way that the Burnouts, as she calls them, use language.

> The Burnouts are overwhelmingly seen as speaking "un-grammaticaly," that is, as using nonstandard grammar... The use of standard grammar simply signals one's member-ship in and identification with the national mainstream... And as with any symbolic material, the use of nonstandard grammar can reflect rejection of mainstream society and identification with the local non-mainstream community (p.67).

Much of the research done on involuntary minorities also highlights the use of non-Standard English or a different language by these students to resist the call for assimilation by the school institution (Fordham, 1999; Lanehart, 1999; Patthey-Chavez, 1993). In her article Dissin' "the Standard': Ebonics as Guerrilla Warfare at Capital High, (1999 #8) Fordham writes about the students:

> Most students at the school resist the requirement that they learn to speak and communicate in "the standard" English dialect, especially in the school context. Their resistance to this state-approved curriculum requirement is their way of "dissin'" or disrespecting this dialect. Thus, dissin' the stan-dard is at the core of the guerrilla warfare at the school and is fundamentally revealed in both the students' refusal to discontinue their use of Ebonics as the language of commu-nication while at or in school and their wholesale avoidance of the standard dialect in most other contexts (p. 273).

The Sidelines data also revealed that the most salient com-monalities uniting the group were marginalization and language. When asked what all of the students in the Sidelines classroom had in common, a student replied, "We have all been kicked out of school and most of us spoke Spanish" (Sidelines student).

Establishing the existence of an oppositional sub-culture in schools defined by marginalization and language explained the Sidelines students' tendency to resist academic events; how-ever, it did not explain the fact that these students came to school faithfully, did a portion of their assignments, and consistently maintained a desire to graduate from a mainstream high school. Recent socio-cultural identity theory sheds light on this contradiction. When viewed from a socio-cultural perspective, identity is situational and context specific (Gee, 1990; Rosaldo, 1989). This is not to say that a person's understanding of herself as Chinese for instance, ever changes; it is just to say that, depending on the context, different aspects of one's identity may be more salient and/or useful. For example, an African-American teen parent may behave more like a student than a mother or vice versa depending on the demands of the situation. Fernie (1993) explains situational identity in terms of positionings:

> These refer to possible ways of being and to each person's experience of those possibilities as they are made available through specific discourses and contexts. Individuals take themselves up as individuals through various discourses (along with the inevitable contradictions among them) as they are made available in spoken and written form. Some subject positionings are made available to some individuals and not to others, depending on the ways in which the subject positionings are understood with respect to gender, ethnicity, class and so on. Individuals (1) take up the various position-ings made available to them as their own (which has come to signify in the modern conception of the individual, who they are, or who they take themselves to be or are taken to be), and (2) resist the positionings they do not want... (p. 98).

Mehan (1994) in his study on the AVID program and Fordham in her study at Capital high found that students who were members of an oppositional culture, but were also academically successful maintained a "dual identity."

> While some AVID students submerged their academic identity entirely, most students maintained dual identities, one at school and one in the neighborhood. Because classes at school segregated them it was not difficult to keep the two peer groups separate. At school, they were free to compete academically; at home in the afternoon, they would assume a different posture (p. 106–07).

Mehan (et al.1994) labels the strategies that students with dual identities use to be academically successful while maintaining their peer group status, border-crossing strategies. The research thus far, however, only addresses border crossing in terms of individual student efforts. As I continued to explore the intersection of student desire to succeed and oppositional resistance, the Sidelines data showed that border-crossing strategies are not limited to individuals. The data show the students using a strategy I call "social permission" to access class events as a group. "Social permission" essentially creates space in which the cultural norms of opposition are temporarily suspended, and everyone in class is required to participate. In this way the social status of individual members is protected.

Methodology

Because language is used as a marker of "social difference," it corresponds that students who want to pursue academic success without giving up their peer affiliations might chose to communicate in "peer code" during class activities. Everhart (1983) asserts, "How the student responds to the teacher communicates to peers who the student is and his or her social relationships with peers." One must consider that language usage often serves several functions at once; furthermore, the separate simultaneous functions of language use need not be in agreement. "Some of these voices may be competing with each other or representing conflicting interests or ideologies" (Jaworski & Coupland, 1999, p. 9). Because of the specific connection between language and sub-culture boundaries among oppositional students, I decided to look for group border-crossing strategies through a discourse analysis of code switching that occurred in the classroom. For this analysis, code switching is a lingual shift from Standard English to any dialect/language that corresponds to the oppositional group "peer code." Code switching also includes use of another language or dialect at any given point in the classroom without an actual mid-sentence shift (Gumperz, 1989, p. 9).

In order to examine the code switching that occurred in the classroom, I revisited the running records of the classes that were videotaped and looked for incidents where code switching occurred. When I found incidents of code switching, I revisited the videotape at that particular moment and transcribed all of the audible classroom talk and visible non-verbal body gestures or cues. The transcripts included a column on the left where specific peer-code words are recorded when the peer code is used. I did this form of analysis to examine the effect of code switching on classroom interaction.

Findings

The following transcripts are taken from a class in which the teacher was introducing the students to the song "Amazing Grace," and the history of how and why it was written. In transcript A the teacher is trying to tell the students about the song. In Transcript B the teacher is trying to get the students to be quiet so that they can listen to the music.

At any given time in the classroom there were two conversational spaces. The Communal Floor was a space that was open to both students and the teacher. If a comment was open to response by anyone in the class, regardless of to whom it may have been directed, a person would speak loud enough to be heard by everyone. The other space was the Private Floor. The Private Floor was a space for private conversations occurring between two or three proximal students, and it was not open to the teacher. Whether or not the Private Floor was operant depended on the perceived importance by the students of what was said on the Communal Floor. For the purpose of analysis, I only transcribed the speech that occurred on the Communal Floor. In the transcript I record the occurrence of Private Floor talk as "consistent murmur." These transcripts reveal three things that are imperative to understanding the border-crossing strategies of a group of oppositional students: 1) The teacher is not, in fact, in control of whether or not students speak on the Communal or Private Floors; 2) Oppositional students are more likely to respond positively to commands given in peer code; and 3) Peer-code commands given by oppositional students to their peers do not always require resistance to learning.

Beginning with point number one: the teacher is not in control of the Communal or Private Floor. In Transcript A the teacher tries nine times to gain control of the Communal Floor in lines 1, 2, 4, 8, 9, 11, 15, 17, and 18. The transcript shows that the students do not actually give up control of the Communal Floor until they are commanded to do so by a peer in peer code on line 20. In Transcript B, a similar phenomenon occurs. The teacher tries to gain control of the Communal Floor four times in lines 3, 5, 19, and 20, but does not succeed until a student demands quiet in peer code in lines 23 and 28. The teacher's lack of access to the Communal Floor is made more explicit in this transcript when Cesar in line 28, following the peer-code command to shut up, lets the teacher know that it is his turn to speak by saying, "Go [Teacher]," as he points his open palm at him. What can be seen in these instances is that despite their desire to learn, as members of an oppositional sub-culture, the students cannot align themselves with the mainstream expectations of behavior by allowing the teacher to control the Communal and/or Private Floors. Therefore, in order to maintain and display their allegiance to their cultural group and participate in class, the students can only respond to commands in peer code. The peer-code command gives the students "social permission" to participate in class without jeopardizing their social status. Until "social permission" to participate in class is given, it is not safe for the students to participate in the way that the teacher would like.

We can deal with the second and third points together: 2) Oppositional students are more likely to respond positively to commands given in peer code; and 3) Peer-code commands given by oppositional students to their peers do not always require resistance to learning. Corresponding to the ethnic diversity of the class members the peer code occurred in two languages, non-Standard English and non-Standard Spanish. Likewise, corresponding to the fact that the majority of the students in the class were Latino Spanish speakers, the transcripts demonstrated that the Spanish peer-code behavior commands were more effective. A student responded with the following when asked about the use of Spanish in the classroom:

> Yea,... and like in Spanish cause most of the time we would talk in Spanish like the serious stuff we talked about we would talk in Spanish because...so when we said like, "Callate," it was more serious (Sidelines student).

The fact that the Spanish peer code is more effective amongst the students is shown in both transcripts. In Transcript

A the command to be quiet is given by a student twice. The first time the command is given is on line 14 by Emmanuel in English. Unlike the lack of any response to the teacher's request, the noise in the class begins to soften. It is not until the command to be quiet is given in Spanish peer code on line 20, however, that the Communal Floor is actually given up by the students so that the teacher can talk.

Transcript B is equally as revealing. Cesar gives the command to be quiet on line 51 in Standard English and receives no response from his peers. On line 52 a student follows with a loud command in Spanish peer code, and all except two students who whisper get quiet. On line 54 Cesar tells the teacher to speak. Thus far we have seen the same thing that happened in Transcript A. What is particularly revealing in this transcript about the strength of the peer code is what happens in lines 56 and 57. The only student in the class who spoke on the Communal Floor after Cesar gave it to the teacher was the non-Spanish speaking African-American student. In line 56, not understanding the seriousness of the Spanish peer-code command for everyone to "shut up," Jamal says, "Enchiladas," making fun of the fact that he does not speak Spanish. In line 57 Cesar essentially translates the Spanish command into a peer code that Jamal will understand by saying, "Shut up fool, damn." Following lines 56 and 57 there is a full moment of complete silence in the room as the students wait for the teacher to speak.

The facts that the Spanish peer code was more effective with Latino students, English peer code was more effective with English-speaking students, and Standard English was not effective at all, regardless of who was speaking, shows that for oppositional students "social permission" to participate in class must come in the code that corresponds to their particular sub-culture and thus substantiates the point that for oppositional students "disobedience" is a cultural requirement. Most pertinent in these findings is that we see the language of "resistance" being used as a means for border crossing for an entire class of oppositional students. Ironically, without negotiation in this language of "resistance," border crossing does not, in fact, occur.

Conclusion, Implications for Practice, and Further Research

The point of this research has been to disrupt the general common sense and theoretical view that the teacher is in complete control of the class. I specifically chose to place the students' speech on the left of the transcript because according to Ochs (1979) people who read from left to right read with the bias that the left-most speaker is the speaker controlling the conversation. These transcripts demonstrate that what occurs during class time is actually negotiated between the students and the teacher. The teacher's waiting, as a result of student discourse, demonstrates his lack of control over whether or not a classroom event would even occur and much less over whether or not the students would actually engage with the content. On the other hand, the transcripts also show that it was in response to the teacher's waiting to be given access to the Communal Floor that the "social permission" commands by the students were given. It is important for practitioners to recognize that class time is not in reality teacher governed, but co-constructed through discourse negotiations both in student-to-student and student-to-teacher interactions. This research shows that it is a self-defeating mistake to disregard the necessity of student-student negotiations, particularly with members of oppositional sub-cultures. The idea of classroom management then should be less about maintaining a controlled, quiet classroom and more about insightfully and carefully managing and facilitating the discoursal negotiations that combine to construct the classroom environment.

More specifically, when constructing a class with members of oppositional sub-cultures, the Sidelines data suggests that it is crucial for teachers to understand that oppositional identity is a collective identity. To be oppositional is to hold allegiance to a group of people who have been marginalized. Oppositional students who do not complete class work or consistently make the choice to misbehave, maybe deciding whether or not to remain in the world as they have know it, or venture into new, possibly very hostile terrain, by changing their identity and joining a different social group. Therefore, in practical terms for instance, it may be a mistake for teachers to deal with disobedience in a classroom on an individual level; it may be more effective for a teacher to look for the root of the problem in what has been constructed in the discourse between the students. Likewise, when dealing with oppositional students, it may be wise for one to consider that disempowerment is one of the most acute issues that these students face; hence, in interactions with oppositional students what the teacher believes are simple classroom management strategies, may be perceived by the students as a continuation of the general society's/school's efforts to disempower. It follows then that such an understanding may force the students, according to their cultural norms, to continue to oppose the teacher and class events. Respecting the students' need for things like "social permission," which only occur in student-to-student interactions, may give the students a sense of empowerment, thus making the display of opposition less necessary.

It is important for practitioners to understand that, despite their cultural frame of reference in opposition to mainstream culture/school, ultimately like any other human being oppositional students also want to succeed, and they do as a group make efforts to do so. It is these group efforts to cross academic/identity borders that practitioners need to gain a deeper understanding of in order to help oppositional students gain access to schooling. Simply labeling the manifestation of oppositional identity as disobedience alleviates the school of its responsibility to educate all students. It is time for us as a nation to move beyond disobedience.

References

Brake, M. (1985). *Comparative youth culture*. London: Routledge Kegan Paul.

Eckert, P. (1989). *Jocks and burnouts social categories and identity in the high school*. New York: Teachers College Press.

Everhart, R. (1983). *Reading, writing, and resistance*. Boston: Routledge and Kegan Paul.

Fernie, D., Bronwyn, D., Kantor, R., & McMurray, P. (1993). Becoming a person in the preschool: Creating integrated gender, school culture, and peer culture positionings. *Qualitative Studies in Education*, 6(2), 95–110.

Fordham, S. (1988). Racelessness as a factor in black students' school success: Pragmatic strategy or pyrrhic victory. *Harvard Educational Review*, 58(1), 54–83.

Fordham, S. (1999). Dissin' "the Standard": Ebonics as guerrilla warfare at Capital High. *Anthropology and Education Quarterly*, 30(3), 272–293.

Fordham, S., & Ogbu, J. U. (1986). Black student's school success: "Coping with the burden of 'acting white.'" *The Urban Review*, 18(3), 176–205.

Gee, J. P. (1990). Social linguistics and literacies: Ideology in discourse. New York: Falmer.

Green, J., & Meyer, L. (1991). The embeddedness of reading in classroom life: Reading as a situated process. In L. A. Baker Carolyn D. (Ed.), *Towards a critical sociology of reading pedagogy*. (Vol. 19, pp. 141–160). Philadelphia: John Benjamins Publishing Co.

Gumperz, J. J. (1989). Linguistic variability in interactional perspective. In W. Kallmeyer (Ed.), *Language usage in Mannheim*. Mannheim: Institute of German Language.

Jaworski, A. C. N. (1999). Perspectives on discourse analysis. In A. J. N. Coupland (Ed.), *The Discourse Reader* (pp. 1–44). New York: Routledge.

Lanehart, S. (1999). African-american vernacular english. In J. A. Fishman (Ed.), *Handbook of language and ethnic identity* (pp. 211–225). New York: Oxford University Press.

Matute-Bianchi, M. E. (1986). Ethnic identities and patterns of school success and failure among Mexican-descent and Japanese-American students in a California high school: An ethnographic analysis. *American Journal of Education* (November), 233–255.

Mehan, H., Hubbard, L., & Villanueava, I. (1994). Forming academic identities: Accommodation without assimilation among involuntary minorities. *Anthropology and Education Quarterly*, 25(2), 91–117.

Ochs, E. (1979). Transcription as theory. In E. S. Ochs, B. B. (Ed.), *Developmental pramatics* (pp. 43–72). New York: Academic.

Ogbu, J. U. (1985). Research currents: Cultural-ecological influence on minority school learning. *Language Arts*, 62(8), 860–869.

Ogbu, J. U. (1992). Adaptation to minority status and impact on school success. *Theory into Practice*, 31(4), 271–296.

Ogbu, J. U. (1995). Cultural problems in minority education: Their interpretations and consequences—part two: Case studies. *The Urban Review*, 27(4).

Patthey-Chavez, G. G. (1993). High school as an arena for cultural conflict and acculturation for Latino Anglelinos. *Anthropology and Education Quarterly*, 24(1), 33–60.

Rosaldo, R. (1989). *Culture and truth: The remaking of social analysis.* Boston: Beacon Press.

Appendix

Transcript A

1 minute of classroom time
Each row equals a moment of speech
Speech that overlaps with the prior speaker's words is placed in brackets [ ].
English translation of Spanish peer code is placed in {} underneath the Spanish words in the first column

Use of Peer Code in Communal Talk	Student Talk	Student non-verbals	Teacher Talk	Teacher non-verbals
1	S: consistent murmur	David and Donald Jamal &? Emmanuel writing/drawing Aaron writing/drawing	Right ok, so check that out.	Standing front, right
2	Consistent murmur		Jamal	Looking at Jamal
3	Ernie: whhii Students: consistent murmur			Waiting
4	Consistent murmur		So Jamal did you hear what Nicole [said]	Pointing to Nicole
5	Ceasar: [Oooh] say can you seeee by the dawn's early light Students: consistent murmur			Looking at Jamal
6	Students: consistent murmur Jamal: I couldn't hear [inaudible]	Jamal: points across the room towards Ceasar		Looking at Jamal
7	Jamal: I didn't stand a chance Students: consistent murmur	Consistent tapping noise in the background		Looking at Jamal
8	Consistent murmur	Consistent tapping	I know its quite hard to hear with [inaudible]	Hand waves across the room
9	Students: consistent murmur	Consistent tapping	So, so more people	Waiting
10	Students: consistent murmur	Consistent tapping		Waiting
11		Consistent tapping	More people	
12 *damn*	Student: damn Consistent murmur	Consistent tapping		Waiting
13	Students: consistent murmur	Consistent tapping		Waiting
14 *fools*	Emmanuel: eh, fools be quiet already Consistent murmur softens but continues	Consistent tapping		Waiting

15	Consistent murmur	Consistent tapping Student starts to whistle	Traffic, you know we don't need to live in L.A. to experience traffic we get it [inaudible]	Head nods
16	Consistent murmur Aaron: if you want to hear traffic go turn on the radio	Consistent tapping		Waiting
17	Consistent murmur	Consistent tapping	So more people, Nicole said	
18	Consistent murmur Emmanuel: stop, stop	Consistent tapping Emmanuel: turned around to look behind him	Uh probably know the words (pause)	
19	Consistent murmur Student: stop,stop	Consistent tapping		Waiting
20 *Callate La Bocas* {Shut up}	Student: Callate La Bocas	Tapping stops		Waiting
21			So more people sing or know the words to Amazing Grace than America's national Anthem, so check that out, ok I don't, I can't say that I have these words memorized but I do know it	

Transcript B

Each row equals a moment of speech
1 minute of classroom time
Speech that overlaps with the prior speaker's words is placed in brackets [].
English translation of Spanish peer code is placed in {} underneath the Spanish words in the first column

Use of Peer Code in Communal Talk	Student Talk	Student non-verbals	Teacher Talk	Teacher non- verbals
31	Oscar: could we hear that - one CD that I wanted to hear E			Walking toward tape at front left
32	Student: Please			Standing by the tape
33			No cause that's not what we are doing	
34	Ceasar: but E- that's gospel [music]			
35	David: [I don't] want to hear that gospel crap Consistent murmur starts		Yea, but another time	Shaking his head
36 *fool*	Ceasar: [ohhh, shut up fool] Consistent murmur			Waiting
37	Ceasar: E- he said [gospel crap] Consistent murmur	Ceasar points at David		Waiting Leans on the desk by the tape
38	Jamal: [I get to hear gospel music] all the time. That's all my mom listens to Consistent murmur			Waiting

39		Donald: it's Christian		Bending over to
		Consistent murmur		fix the tape
40		Ceasar: [he said I don't wanna		Fixing the tape
		listen to gospel crap.]		
		Deedee: [that's what my		
		grandmother listens to]		
		Consistent murmur		
41		David: I'm not Christian		Fixing the tape
		young lady		
		Consistent murmur		
42		Jamal: [what are you?] Aaron: turning to look at David		Leaning back on
		Aaron: [that's Christian?]		the desk
		Consistent murmur		
43		David: I don't know		Waiting
44		Aaron: [that's Christian Aaron: still looking toward		Waiting
		music, man, gospel] David and Ceasar		
		Student: [oooohhhh]		
45		David: yea		Waiting
46		DeeDee: yea, gospel		Waiting
		music is Christian		
47		Aaron: throw that [away]		Waiting
48			[so you] need to	Waiting
			listen up. ok	
49		Students: laughing and Jamal: throwing his arms in the air And the words		Waiting
yo wat up man		talking [inaudible] Ceasar: looking at David and smiling		
		Student: [inaudible] DeeDee: looking toward David		
		you Aaron Ana: looking toward David		
		David: Aaron yo wat Oneal: looking toward David.		
		up man David puts his hand in the air and bends		
		Consistent murmur his wrist so his hand is parallel to the		
			desk while looking at Aaron	
50		Consistent murmur Emmanuel: drawing		Waiting
singing rapping		Student: singing/ Most other students looking		
		rapping back and forth		
		Ernie: E, E, I know between David and E-		
		the whole song		
51		Ceasar: you guys please		Puts his head
		listen		down
52		Student: Callate la Bocas		Waiting
callate la bocas		Consistent murmur softens		
{shut up}				
53		Student whispers and		Waiting
callate la bocas		chuckles: Callate la bocas		
{shut up}		Ana: talking softly		
54		Ceasar: go E		Waiting
55		Student: gracias		Waiting
Gracias				
{thanks}				
56		Jamal: Enchiladas		Waiting
Enchiladas				
{Enchiladas are a				
well known				
traditional Mexican				
Food}				

57	Ceasar loud whisper: Be		Waiting
fool	quiet fool, damn		
	Go [Teacher].		
58		All eyes are on E		Staring/waiting
59		All eyes still on E	So the music...	

"FICTIVE IMAGININGS": CONSTRUCTING BIRACIAL IDENTITY AND SENNA'S *CAUCASIA*

CARINA A. EVANS

UNIVERSITY OF CALIFORNIA, SANTA BARBARA

"The emergence of a racially mixed population is transforming the 'face' of the United States" (Root 3).

"Check it out. Welcome to the land of miscegenation" (Senna 11).

Imagining America as a "land of miscegenation" forecasts a diverse, multiracial future—the melting pot of cliché and myth. Yet I approach this issue with personal interest, because I am part of the growing biracial population that researcher Maria Root predicts will "transform the face" of America. In order to imagine this multiracial future, we must also consider its divided origin and the process of transformation that led to contemporary understandings of race and mixed race identity. This paper seeks to trace the history of biracial identity, from its first inception as a colonialist construct to its current re-imagining in post-modern America. Through an examination of race and its function throughout history, we can better understand the contested position of biracial identity. I argue that literature plays an active role in constructing these racial myths, which makes the question of biracial literature even more relevant. As an example, I turn to Danzy Senna's first novel *Caucasia*, a story about a teenager struggling to define herself racially. *Caucasia*, like the projected multiracial future, requires a new mode of thinking about biracial identity. These possibilities are dependent upon a subversion of historical constructions of racial identity and a reinterpretation of what it means to be biracial. Beyond the limitations imposed by our racial past, *Caucasia* participates in the writing of a reinvigorated racial future.

I. The Social Construction of Ethnicity

This examination begins with the hypothesis that race and ethnicity are social constructs, established by various historical processes and replicated through continued social practice. Werner Sollors makes a similar argument in the introduction to *The Invention of Ethnicity*, in which he uses the word "invention" to suggest a process of creation or construction in thinking about race and ethnicity: "The forces of modern life embodied by such terms as 'ethnicity,' 'nationalism,' or 'race' can indeed be meaningfully discussed as 'inventions'" (xi). Sollors's argument that racial identity can be "invented" radically contradicts essentialist notions about cultural identity, meaning that there is nothing fundamentally *black* about being black. In order to prove this, Sollors writes, "It is not any a priori cultural *difference* that makes ethnicity" (xvi). If there is no "a priori cultural difference" that creates ethnicity, it also must be asserted that there is no meaningful biological difference.[1] And with no biological or cultural foundations, it would appear as though the basic category would collapse; how can race continue to be meaningful if the essentialist notions that define it have been deflated? The answer is simple: despite the fact that race can be acknowledged as a construct, we must not forget that it carries very real social implications.

II. The History of the Social Construction of Ethnicity

In order to understand these social implications, we can look to the history of racial discourse in the United States. In his book *Colonial Desire: Hybridity in Theory, Culture and Race*, Robert Young acknowledges that much of the discourse on race emerged from the initial moments of contact between "colonizer and colonized, self and Other, with the second only knowable through a necessarily false representation, a Manichean division that threatens to reproduce the static, essentialist categories it seeks to undo" (5). Young recognizes that colonial racial discourse constructs two distinct groups—European and Other—which confirm supposed essential differences as lived reality. Out of necessity, according to Young, it became important to think of "European" as a category of unified, uniform people, clearly distinguishable from "Orientals" or Africans: "Europeans and Africans, say, were clearly of different species, the question became more difficult with respect to Europeans themselves. Did not Europe itself provide examples of hybrid races?" (16). Yet, despite the intra-group mixings amongst Europeans, they transformed themselves into "imagined communit[ies] of homogeneous national identit[ies]," a need generated by colonial contact (17). However, Young's discussion of uniform European-ness, which comes to define "whiteness," forms just one half of the history of ethnicity as a social construct.

The construction of the racial Other is just as much rooted in colonial contact as is the construction of what would eventually come to be known as white. The Other is an embodiment of the anti-European—dark, uncivilized, heathen; Other includes both Africans kidnapped as part of the slave system and indigenous people cruelly forced into colonization. Because the relationship between Europeans and the colonial Other was one of power and domination, master and slave, strict definitions between the two groups were required in order to maintain social order. Young identifies this distinction as a "fundamental binary division between black and white," which was justified by European philosophy, religion, and science (180). This division established an asymmetrical power dynamic between whites and blacks (including indigenous people), mapped out according to supposed essential differences.

III. Biracial Identity as a Historical Construct

The construction of biracial[2] identity materialized out of the same racial discourse that solidified "white" and "black" as fixed categories. Racial hybridity, according to Young, was the inevitable result of colonial contact, despite the desire to maintain rigid boundaries between Europeans and the Others. This hybridity, according to Young, was conceptualized as racial "degeneration":

> A culture in its colonial operation becomes hybridized, alienated and potentially threatening to its European original through the production of polymorphously perverse

people who are, in Bhabha's phrase, white, but not quite: in the nineteenth century, this threatening phenomenon of being degraded from a civilized condition was discussed as the process of 'decivilization.' (175)

By using the word "decivilization," Young intends to describe European anxieties about racial mixing, which would continue for centuries beyond the original colonial context. Fear of such impurity resulted in obsessive categorization of "miscegenated, mongrel" people, in order to "track any furtive vestiges of secreted blackness" (Young 177). As proof, Young cites a table describing racial mixing in South America in which "twenty-three crosses can be determined, and have received names" (176).[3] Fixed ideas about what constitutes "white" and what constitutes "black" required that multiracial individuals be categorized according to a hierarchy of racial identity, which cemented in place supposed differences as tangible distinctions that affected social reality.

The fact that multiracial individuals were categorized somewhere in between black and white made their social position correspondingly liminal and at times poorly defined. F. James Davis examines this issue in his book, *Who is Black? One Nation's Definition*, with his discussion of the first step taken to categorize mulattoes and other multiracial individuals as black—the one-drop rule: "The pressure grew to make the legal definition correspond to what had become the customary social definition of a Negro as a person with any degree of black ancestry, and the legislatures and courts began to move in that direction" (34). Consequently, the one-drop rule resulted in a conflation of multiracial people and so-called "pure blacks." However, Davis also notes that in some places in the South, "Instead of being defined as blacks by a one-drop rule, free mulattoes became a third class, between blacks and whites" (35). It is especially important to note how the construction of this third class affected lived reality; positioned between blacks and whites, this elite class "enjoyed more privileges than unmixed blacks, but fewer than those enjoyed by whites" (37).[4] The collapse of the slavery system and Reconstruction, however, again resulted in a conflation of mixed race people with unmixed blacks, and the one-drop rule became almost universal in identifying who could be categorized as black.

This historical construction of biracial identity arose out of specific conditions dictated by colonialism and slavery, a seemingly distant origin with repercussions for each new generation. For example, the eventual disappearance of the third class[5] meant that multiracial people had to "pass" as white in order to enjoy continued privilege. Sollors explains the phenomenon of passing as a mode of survival: "Racial passing is particularly a phenomenon of the nineteenth and the first half of the twentieth century ... perhaps most important, only a situation of sharp inequality between groups would create the need for the emergence of a socially significant number of cases of passing" (*Neither* 248). Even if passing was a means of surviving social inequality, it carried with it negative associations of its own—danger, isolation, and depression. Of course, the alternative to passing was being subsumed by blackness, which had been expanded to include individuals with just "one drop" of black blood. Many biracial individuals simply became "black" if they hadn't already thought of themselves in this way, resulting in the disappearance of mixed race as its own class.

IV. Narrative and Racial Ideology

Throughout this brief history of race and mixed race in America, literature plays an important role in fabricating racial ideology, revealing a close relationship between narrative and the world. According to Hayden White, "Narrative is an expression in discourse of a distinct mode of experiencing and thinking about the world, its structures, and its processes" (59). In this way, narrative is an active medium that participates in both ideology and the creation of history. James Phelan calls this the "ideology of narrative texts...that is such things as the interests served, the values expressed, the power relations reinforced or challenged by a given narrative" (132). Narratives communicate ideology through form and technique, though Phelan is quick to caution, "We cannot separate technique from the larger experience it contributes to" (138). Therefore, in order to think about how narrative participates in the construction of ethnic identity, we must think about the concept of an ethnic project and analyze the creation of so-called racialized literatures.

By use of the term "ethnic project," I mean to imply the project of constructing ethnic identity in literary texts, which are both informed by racial ideology and actively working to make new contributions. Sollors asks two particularly relevant questions about the role literature plays in this process: "What is the active contribution literature makes, as a productive force, to the emergence and maintenance of communities by reverberation and of ethnic distinctions...How is the illusion of ethnic 'authenticity' stylistically created in a text?" (*Invention* xiv). However, Sollors's answers to his questions bring us no closer to thinking about the "stylistic creation" of ethnicity. As one possible answer, he vaguely suggests, "It is the ethnic text's ability to generate the sense of difference out of a shared cultural context" (xvi). What is implied here by "shared cultural context," and how is this concretely mobilized by literature? In order to answer these questions, I want to return to my previous discussion in which I presented the argument that we might look to the form or technique of narrative in order to analyze its relationship to ideology. In the same way, I would suggest that Sollors is advocating a study of particular narrative elements, including content. If we were thinking about what makes a black text *black*, for example, we might consider such things as the use of language, popular culture, character, setting, and history, in constructing the illusion of black authenticity. Therefore, ethnic texts construct ethnicity by communicating ideology—essential notions about individual and group identities—through narrative discourse.

V. Biracial Literature

When I ask what makes a black text *black*, there is the appearance of understanding what is meant by *black*—the same "shared cultural context" described by Sollors. However, there is some ambiguity when I apply the same question to biracial literature. Applying the same model describing the relationship between narrative and ideology, we can say that a biracial text is biracial in its treatment of racial ideology about mixed race identity. Thus, the literature is informed by the long history previously mapped out in this paper, and it continues to solidify our understandings of how this identity is constructed. In an interesting move, however, Sollors addresses the question with a much more concrete understanding of what constitutes biracial (or interracial, as he labels it) literature: "By 'interracial literature' I mean...works in all genres that represent love and family relations involving black-white couples, biracial individuals, their descendants, and their larger kin—to all of whom the phrasing may be applied, be it as couples, as individuals, or as larger family units" (*Neither* 3). Here, Sollors attaches a biological basis to his definition, even while admitting that he is critical of imagining such a foundation in constructing ethnicity. However, Sollors is not incorrect in his alignment of "interracial literature" with the same albeit false constructions of what constitutes multiracial identity.

In order to analyze how mixed race identity is constructed in literature, we ought to turn to narrative theory for a better understanding of narrative elements at work. If we consider the body of biracial literature as a whole, there are particular similarities that emerge as significant—the ideas of *passing*, phenotypic racial marking, corrupted blood, insider/outsider status, etc. These patterns suggest the larger presence of masterplots[6] functioning in these texts. Porter Abbott defines the concept of a masterplot as the following: "There are stories that we tell over and over in myriad forms and that connect vitally with our deepest values, wishes, and fears" (36). Using an example of a common masterplot, Abbott sets forth the Cinderella story, which has been reinvented and reinterpreted many times throughout literary history. However, Abbott also suggests that masterplots can be more culturally specific than universal stories like Cinderella, meaning that we might say that biracial literature has a unique story of its own to tell.

One such masterplot that allows us entry into the literature is the cliché tragic mulatto story. If masterplots "connect vitally with our deepest values, wishes, and fears" as Abbott argues, the tragic mulatto masterplot says much about the construction of mixed race identity. Remembering that multiracial individuals were constructed historically as degenerate, uncivilized progeny, the transformation into "tragic" literary figures makes sense. Though there are many variations on the plot, the basic idea is as follows:

1. The tragic mulatto is positioned between black and white, and is often the recipient of both privilege and scorn.

2. This person is read as racially ambiguous, and often fulfills "white" standards of beauty (having good hair, fair skin, etc.).

3. Consequently, appearance enables this person to engage in forms of passing depending upon social situations.

4. Occupying liminal space, however, carries fatal implications. Often, the tragic mulatto suffers either literal or metaphorical death.

For examples of the tragic mulatto masterplot, we can look to numerous multiracial texts: Chesnutt's *House Behind the Cedars*, Larsen's *Passing*, Brown's *Clotel* and even texts by our most famous American authors like Faulkner's *Light in August*. It is accurate to say that the "tragedies" suffered by the characters in these novels vary in their degree; however, the idea of the mixed race person as tragic is constant from text to text. In fact, this tragedy is expected by readers of biracial literature as an essential part of the genre. Peter Rabinowitz explains the anticipation of certain narrative conventions endemic to particular genres: "Western readers' prior knowledge of conventions of reading shapes their experiences and evaluations of the narratives they confront" (3). This prior knowledge of convention especially shapes how narratives experience closure; according to Abbott, once readers recognize the kind of narrative sequence they are reading, they expect an ending according to their experiences with prior texts (47). Thus readers of multiracial literature expect tragedy to shape the narrative, because mixed race identity has been constructed as such and other texts have perpetuated the claim.

VI. Re-imagining Biracial Literature Through Caucasia

Senna's *Caucasia*, however, is positioned to take on the construction in ways previous narratives were not able to do. Despite the history of race beginning with colonialism and leading up to the early part of the twentieth century, many of the categories that were formerly thought of as fixed are now being called into question. With the advent of the Civil Rights Movement, consciousness about multiracial identity began to develop, especially with the sudden increase of a racially mixed population in the

United States. Root describes this phenomenon in the following passage:

> The 'biracial baby boom' in the United States started about 25 years ago, around the time the last laws against miscegenation (race mixing) were repealed in 1965. The presence of racially mixed persons defies the social order predicated upon race, blurs racial and ethnic group boundaries, and challenges generally accepted proscriptions and prescriptions regarding intergroup relations. Furthermore, and perhaps most threatening, the existence of racially mixed persons challenges long-held notions about the biological, moral, and social meaning of race. (3)

Root's argument suggests that the visibility of biracial and multiracial individuals will force the collapse of antiquated ethnic constructions. Indeed, their presence has already begun to reshape the way we think about mixed race identity; it is no longer tragic or merely subsumed by other racial categories. This re-imagining has seeped into literature as well, which is evident in Sollors's assessment of the demise of passing: "Passing was swept aside in social history by the civil rights movement, and in literature by the combined successes of Zora Neale Hurston and Richard Wright, who no longer employed the theme" (*Neither* 284). As yet another example, the novel *Caucasia* emerges out of this sense of post-Civil Rights Era optimism to construct a new sense of biracial identity—new in that it aggressively takes on the vestiges of the old.

Senna's work first does this by undermining classic conventions of multiracial literature. Passing, for example, carries less of the tragic tone associated with classic texts; Senna's world is open to racial play and reinterpretation, demonstrating that no identity is fixed. In this text, passing is more like a racial performance in which Birdie, Senna's protagonist, can costume herself at will. Her first attempt to be "black," for example, occurs when she buys new clothing to wear to the all-black private school, Nkrumah:

> I learned the art of changing at Nkrumah, a skill that would later become second nature to me ... I started wearing my hair in a tight braid to mask its texture. I had my ears pierced and convinced my mother to buy me a pair of gold hoops like the other girls at school wore ... On one weekend

shopping spree at Tello's, with my sister shouting orders to me, I bought a pair of Sergio Valente jeans, a pink vest, a jean jacket with sparkles on the collar, and spanking-white Nike sneakers. (63)

In this excerpt, clothing represents black urban culture, and Birdie marks herself as black by participating in consumerism and buying these items. Birdie even plays with black speech as a way of completing the illusion: "I stood many nights in front of the bathroom mirror, practicing how to say 'nigger' the way kids in school did it, cropping the 'er' so that it became not a slur, but a term of endearment: *nigga*" (63). By taking on this image, Birdie is read as black by others at the school and finds a peer group: "It took a while, but sometime late that fall at Nkrumah, my work paid off...Finally Maria spoke, 'So you black?' I nodded slowly, as if unsure of it myself" (63). This passage describes hesitancy within Birdie to identify completely with black culture, demonstrating her recognition of complex racial identity. The trappings of blackness fail to make Birdie black, since the reader is aware of a real, unchanged Birdie beneath the costume.

A similar situation occurs when Birdie passes as white; her racial performance perfected at Nkrumah permits her to slip easily into a new white identity. Again, clothing and makeup act as camouflage: "From the outside, it must have looked like I was changing into one of those New Hampshire girls. I talked the talk, walked the walk, swayed my hips to the sound of heavy metal, learned to wear blue eyeliner and frosted lipstick and snap my gum" (233). In this passage, certain cultural identifiers are attached to whiteness: heavy metal music, blue eyeliner, frosted lipstick, and bubble gum. Birdie even absorbs white speech as part of her performance: "Sometimes I got carried away with my fantasy and would start talking differently, affectedly, trying to imitate Libby's long nasal drawl, and using expressions I had heard Nicholas use, as if they were my own. Fuckwit. Loser. Awesome. Bummer" (194). Much like Birdie imitates black speech, she also mimics the white voices around her. Birdie's performance of whiteness, however, is just performance. For example, she describes whiteness as something that threatens the real Birdie: "It made me feel a little contaminated. I wondered if whiteness were contagious. If it were, then surely I had caught it.

I imagined this 'condition' affected the way I walked, talked, dressed, danced, and at its most advanced stage, the way I looked at the world and at other people" (329). By terming whiteness a "condition," Birdie disassociates herself from her performance of various racial markers. This discomfort with identifying as either black or white reveals a turning away from historical attitudes and a need to reconsider the category of biracial.

The recognition and subversion of false racial categories is one way of engaging in this process. *Caucasia* argues that subversive possibility exists in the ability to re-imagine and reinvent. Birdie remarks that passing put her "in a perpetual state of reinvention" and allowed her to be a "fictive imagining" of possible identities: "In those years, I felt myself to be incomplete—a gray blur, a body in motion, forever galloping toward completion—half a girl, half-caste, half-mast, and half-baked, not quite ready for consumption. And for me, there was comfort in that state of incompletion" (137). Birdie's words acknowledge the fact that she is comfortable in the space of the in-between—the gray between black and white beyond historical racial categories. The *essential* Birdie, whoever lies beneath performance and play, is outside of color: "There's skin color, eye color, hair color, and then there's invisible color—that color rising above you. It's the color of your soul, and it rests just beyond the skin" (321). Birdie's "invisible color" suggests acceptance of biracial identity, a position with liberating potential and endless racial possibility. Even the name "Birdie" suggests the ability to take flight and transcend limitations.

There is subversive potential not in the idea of racial transcendence, which fits the melting pot model of racial utopia, but in drawing attention to the fragility of racial categories. The future imagined by *Caucasia* is not a world without racial distinctions but a world with limitless racial complexity. History has revealed the limitations of racial ideology; however, present circumstances present the opportunity for re-thinking formerly fixed categories. *Caucasia* is evidence of this revolutionary possibility that we can look forward to seeing in texts still to come, and like Root, I believe that the results "may force us to reexamine our construction of race and the hierarchical social order it supports" (3). By exploding the categories of black and white, biracial identity as it is imagined in *Caucasia* de-essentializes racial identity and generates the possibility of an existence in the gray, a space in which we might come to our own conclusions about racial identity. If literature is our lens for seeing the world, *Caucasia* envisions a world in which individuals actively participate in the creation of their own "fictive imaginings" of race and mixed race, opening a space for meaningful dialogue to begin.

Notes

1. Many works have been written about supposed biological differences between races, some of these writings working to perpetuate racist notions about inferiority and superiority amongst blacks and whites respectively. Davis counters this argument with the explanation, "Human races are subspecies groups, not completely discrete categories, and were so even before miscegenation. The fact that reproduction occurs across racial lines demonstrates that all human beings belong to the same species" (20).

2. For the purposes of this essay, the words "multiracial," "biracial," and "mixed" include individuals with both black and white ancestry, though I am aware of the fact that these words usually encompass more than just these two groups. This analysis of white/black mixing is especially relevant later on when I describe the "tragic mulatto" tradition in literature, leading up to *Caucasia*.

3. Young is citing the work of Johann von Tschudi, published as *Travels in Peru*, and "subsequently widely reproduced in anthropological accounts of race" (175). This table categorizes the various possible crossings between Europeans, Africans, and Indians.

4. Here, I am glossing over an entire history of free people of color, who were especially prevalent in Louisiana. Davis notes, "The mulatto elites avoided identification and marriage with both blacks and whites, following the Haitian pattern, carefully arranging marriages with other mulattoes. The southern Louisiana mulattoes in general developed and preserved the status of an in-between third group that was neither black nor white, thus avoiding the imposition of the one-drop rule until the 1850's" (36). Alongside this system of separateness, however, existed a system of institutionalized mulatto concubinage; in many places, according to Young, "Miscegenation was both widespread and tolerated" (37).

5. I do not mean to imply that the elite completely disappeared, though I would argue that they no longer enjoyed many of the same privileges of being "almost white."

6. Masterplot is almost interchangeable with masternarrative.

Works Cited

Abbott, Porter. *Cambridge Introduction to Narrative.* Draft version of ms.

Davis, F. James. *Who is Black? One Nation's Definition.* University Park: Pennsylvania State UP, 2001.

Phelan, James. "Narrative Discourse, Literary Character, and Ideology." *Reading Narrative: Form, Ethics, Ideology.* Ed. Phelan. Columbus: Ohio State UP, 1989. 132–46.

Rabinowitz, Peter J. *Before Reading: Narrative Conventions and the Politics of Interpretation.* Ithaca: Cornell UP, 1987.

Root, Maria, ed. *Racially Mixed People in America.* Newbury Park, California: Sage Publications, 1992.

Senna, Danzy. *Caucasia.* New York: Riverhead Books, 1999.

Sollors, Werner. *Invention of Ethnicity.* Oxford: Oxford UP, 1991.

—————. *Neither Black Nor White Yet Both: Thematic Explorations of Interracial Literature.* Oxford: Oxford UP, 1997.

White, Hayden. "Storytelling: Historical and Ideological." *Centuries' Ends, Narrative Means.* Ed. Robert Newman. Stanford, California: Stanford UP, 1996. 58–78.

THE BEGINNING

LAURA FURLAN SZANTO

UNIVERSITY OF CALIFORNIA, SANTA BARBARA

It all goes back to that photograph. I must be five or six years old in the picture. I am wearing turquoise Toughskins, a white shirt with Mexican embroidery around the neck, and a full-on headdress—the dimestore tourist kind. The feathers are dyed bright colors, red and blue and yellow, and there are white leather straps hanging down on the sides, weighted by plastic beads and rabbits' feet. I am standing alone in Durango, Colorado. Behind me is a steaming locomotive, and to the right is a donkey, walking down the middle of the gravel main street. My hands are stuffed into my front pockets, and like in all of my childhood photographs, there is a look of defiance on my face.*

It was on this same Durango trip that my family took me to Mesa Verde, a place of deep caves and dusky smells and, reportedly, dead Indians. I walked through the caves, I climbed the ladders. I listened to the tour guide talk about those Indians, but I felt no connection to them. I didn't think that my ancestors lived

---

* The photograph shown here was taken on the same family vacation in 1975. Although I vividly remember the photo with the locomotive in Durango, I cannot physically find it. Even after a thorough search of family albums, it remains undiscovered.

in caves. It just didn't feel right.

I was adopted and raised by a white suburban family in Chicago. My adopted parents knew as much about my Indian heritage as I did: absolutely nothing. I had—and still have—a piece of paper, folded into eighths and smudged in many places—that was my only proof.

This form verified that my biological father was Indian and in the Army. My mother was seventeen. I imagined a million scenarios of who they were, how they met, why they gave me up. I was convinced my father had died in the Vietnam War. Twice at the Memorial in Washington, DC, I scanned the wall for his name. I thought I might feel drawn to it, but I never was.

In college, my roommate would look through her anthropology book, comparing the faces in the photographs to mine. We never could find a perfect match. I went to my first powwow when I was in college, a junior at the University of Iowa. I had never seen so many Indians together in the same place. These people were from nearby Tama. Were we related? I wondered as I watched the dances, looked at the tables full of jewelry, smiled at the vendors, ate fry bread. The drums sounded like a heartbeat.

At Iowa, I enrolled in a American Indian literature course. I had finally made a connection. These authors were Indians like me, and they were alive, somewhere, writing beautiful books. A young man in the class, a Cherokee, showed his CIB to the rest of us. This was something foreign, and I certainly didn't have one— a Certificate of Indian Blood. He was some part of a 32nd. I didn't care about his blood quantum, but I wondered what mine would be.

My parents always reminded me that I was part-Indian. I wasn't sure which part. "You look just like your mother," people would say. Were they just being nice? Granted, I am light-skinned, a mixed-blood from mixed-bloods. People say I was "adopted out." Out of what? Like I was rescued—from savagery, poverty, alcoholism, Indianness. Out of truth, knowledge, heritage, I say. But I was also "adopted in"—into a particular time and place and life I would not have lived. I occupy this strange place between being and not being, out and in, white and red. In the photo, I am the real Indian wearing phony Indian feathers.

LOS ANGELES COUNTY MUSEUM OF ART: LOOKING FORWARD

MELINDA GÁNDARA

UNIVERSITY OF CALIFORNIA, SANTA BARBARA

In recent years, increasing attention has been paid to the role that museums play as cultural arbiters. As competing constituencies importune these institutions with conflicting demands for validation of agendas that are as much social and political as they are aesthetic, museum directors and curators find themselves in a quandary. Because satisfying one interest group often entails displeasing another, administrators are inevitably tempted to occupy themselves with a succession of placatory gestures: a nod here, a bow there—a genuflection toward political correctness, followed by a curtsey in favor of tradition. The end result may be an institution that is perpetually in motion—but going nowhere.

Fortunately, the Los Angeles County Museum of Art (LACMA) has a clearly defined path toward continuing success, and its management has already taken significant steps in this direction. Its sense of purpose is captured with singular clarity in its Mission Statement, which begins with an injunction, "To serve the public," and then prioritizes the elements of its service under the headings "educational, aesthetic, intellectual and cultural."[1] When an institution that is officially described as "the largest general art Museum in the West" chooses to put "educational" before "aesthetic, intellectual, and cultural," it is clearly making a statement.[2] Its significance can be inferred from Andrea Rich's definition of LACMA's educational goal: "To extend the museum experience in the fullest possible way to the widest possible audience, both present and future."[3] In so saying, Rich is acknowledging the fact that art appreciation is more than a casual pastime—and that to experience a museum to the fullest, a visitor requires a significant amount of formally organized prior knowledge.

With this in mind, LACMA is making a significant investment in educational programs "involving the Los Angeles
Unified School District, seven cultural institutions, and four universities."[4] These programs include internship programs, a teachers' academy, partnerships with community-based organizations
like the California African-American Museum and the Latino
Museum of History, Art, and Culture, an experimental gallery
featuring art-making activities, studio and art history classes, and
a multifaceted outreach effort in which thousands of students
and families participate.[5] Most impressively, LACMA recently
committed most of its curatorial resources and exhibition
space—and, by extension, its prestige—to an unapologetically
didactic retrospective show entitled *Made in California: Art, Image,
and Identity, 1900–2000*. Seeking "to place art and artists within a
particular historical, political, social, and economic context,"[6] the
show re-examined a number of immanently controversial issues
by posing two broad, thematic questions: "Which California?"
and "Whose California?"

In response, the more than 1,200 artworks, ephemera, and
other cultural artifacts[7] displayed in the exhibition suggested
answers that were consistently provocative and ineluctably unset-
tling. In a lyrical essay that should be regarded as a work of art in
its own right, Richard Rodriguez captures the essence of the
show's recurring message: "Eureka! (I have found it.) California's
official motto," he proposes, "should be mistranslated: *I have
brought it.*"[8] As the evidence presented by *Made in California*
amply demonstrated, California is *not* a place that reinvents itself;
rather, it is a place that is invented elsewhere—by outsiders—
who are still in the process of arriving. For museum traditional-
ists who see LACMA as the conservator of the state's cultural
heritage, this may be a deeply disturbing idea. For members of
the public at large who are coping with relentless, externally
driven changes in their daily lives, it may be an enlightening
reflection of reality.

Mark Jones, a curator at the British Museum, recently
asserted, "The loss of certainty about what is and what is not
real, and the increasing fictionalization of the past, means that
museums have found themselves acting as psychic anchors."[9] The
critical reaction to *Made in California* suggests that much of the

cultural establishment would prefer to see LACMA serving as a safe harbor, as opposed to becoming an active participant in the state's turbulent milieu. Some reviews were so negative that it seemed as if their authors were not simply displeased by the exhibition, but personally threatened by it. After panning the show in an initial review, Christopher Knight, the art critic for the *Los Angeles Times*, felt compelled to expatiate his attack in a subsequent commentary that accused the exhibition's curators of alienating the museum's core constituency.[10] Amplifying on this theme in a paragraph that fairly drips with condescension, Knight wrote: "Feeling as I do that it is entirely possible to live a long, happy and productive life without ever seeing a painting or sculpture, I've never been one to proselytize for art. Attraction, not promotion, is the preferred methodology, given that attraction claims the most powerful life-altering potential."[11]

From Knight's patrician perspective, the unwashed masses are clearly better off in their bowling leagues. Those among them who are truly worthy, Knight would have us believe, will be attracted by a mysterious force in an unspecified manner to the hallowed halls where the cognoscenti gather to admire Art, with a capital "A." For such nakedly elitist sentiments to be published under the byline of the chief art critic of the leading newspaper in the West is, in a word, mind-boggling. LACMA should take pride in Knight's disapproval; the alternative would be equivalent to a political endorsement from Jesse Helms or Pat Buchanan.

LACMA needs to persevere on the inclusive, educationally-oriented course it has set because it is morally right—and because it is politically pragmatic. Those who are skeptical about this latter assessment are best answered by paraphrasing James Carville's gnomic wisdom from the 1992 Presidential Election: "It's the *demographics*, stupid!" Changes in the composition of California's population have long been anticipated. What was not expected was the speed with which these changes would occur, or the lengths to which they might eventually go.[12] In October 2000, the Los Angeles County Department of Regional Planning projected that the county's Latino population would grow from 3,351,242 in 1990 to 4,503,479 in 2000, an increase of 34.38%.[13] At this level, Latinos would comprise 45.56% of the county's total population. In view of the fact that most projections and surveys tend to underestimate the true size of the Latino community,[14] there is an excellent possibility that Latinos already constitute an absolute majority in Los Angeles County.

In his monograph entitled "Race and Education," Alan Nishio, Associate Vice President for Student Services at California State University, Long Beach, cogently summarized the views of many Latino community leaders when he wrote:

> All education is the major vehicle for gaining economic and social mobility in society. Without that we are stratified—we already are in many ways—but educational opportunity provides avenues of mobility for groups that otherwise would be locked out of those opportunities.[15]

At a recent debate among Los Angeles mayoral candidates, union leader María Elena Durazo restated this point more bluntly: "We need the same education and opportunities as the millionaires of this city."[16] No publicly supported organization that relies in significant measure on the largesse of local taxpayers can afford to ignore this message. According to its Annual Report 1997/98, LACMA derived 26% of its operating income from "County allocation and government grants." Ominously, the same document states that 24% of operating income came from "investment results."[17] If the current downturn in the equity markets proves to be more than temporary, LACMA's dependence on the public purse—and on the goodwill of community leaders who influence how it is disbursed—may turn out to be crucial to its future progress.

As an institution that has committed itself to supporting public education, LACMA has reason to be optimistic about the support it can generate in the Latino community. Unlike a number of other groups, Latinos are inclined to take a positive view of Los Angeles and what it has to offer them. According to a *Los Angeles Times* poll released earlier this month:

> Latinos surveyed in Los Angeles were twice as likely as whites—and much more likely than African Americans—to say quality of life has improved in the last five years ... And more than half of Latinos surveyed rated public school education as adequate or excellent. By contrast, a majority of whites and seven in 10 blacks said schools were inadequate or very poor. The positive appraisal among

Latinos persists even though *Latino children, who represent 70% of L.A.'s public school enrollment,* often endure the longest bus rides to school and the worst overcrowding.[18] (emphasis added)

LACMA has every reason to expect that the educational contributions it makes will be recognized by this community and, if appropriately handled, be acknowledged by its leadership in ways that will assist the museum in strengthening and expanding its programs.

A museum, of course, is more than just an amalgamation of programs and artworks; it is also a building—or, in LACMA's case, a collection of buildings. Its Wilshire Boulevard campus has been the site of an incremental, ad hoc expansion over the past forty years that has left it without a coherent focal point or unifying architectural style.[19] Museum director and President Andrea Rich recently commented: "We don't have good circulation. Nobody knows where they are going at LACMA."[20] If ease of navigation were a criterion for museum greatness, then the Metropolitan Museum in New York, the National Gallery in London, and any number of other major institutions would all have to be deemed less than great.[21]

Rich's remarks are a prelude to the consideration of a major new building project at LACMA, an undertaking that trustee Eli Broad sees as "a big opportunity to build a distinguished building by a world-class architect."[22] Rich blithely estimates the cost at "less than $1 billion";[23] Broad, who actually knows what $1 billion looks like, figures it will take "well over $200 million,"[24] and goes on to promise:

> I will be a big financial supporter of the effort, but I can't do it myself. When I'm committed, I would hope that other wealthy individuals and our great foundations, who have been very good to LACMA over many decades, would likewise get committed.[25]

Some twenty years ago, artist Donald Judd offered the following caustic assessment of the motivation for museum building: "Art is only an excuse for the building housing it, which is the real symbol, precise as chalk screeching on a blackboard, of the culture of the new rich."[26] Eli Broad, a real estate developer who was also a prime mover in the campaign to build the Disney

Concert Hall, appears to fit quite readily into Judd's view of the museum world. Broad speaks ardently "about having a vision," touts the importance of "great civic buildings that will inspire other developers," and expresses his admiration for the techno-trademark architectural style of which Frank Gehry is currently a leading practitioner.[27] He is also an old-school plutocrat, a representative of a class of affluent civic leaders who believe they know what is best for Los Angeles (and themselves), and who team up to make it happen. Los Angeles Mayor Richard Riordan, also a wealthy businessman, is another member of this oligarchy and a frequent collaborator of Broad's on civic projects.[28] With Riordan facing mandatory retirement because of term limits, and with Broad's personal net worth diminished by approximately half a billion dollars because of the current stock market downturn,[29] it just may be that the influence of this particular segment of the community has peaked.

In its place, a new coalition of leaders is beginning to assemble. They are no less interested in economic progress, but their vision of what Wilshire Boulevard's *La Milla de Milagro*[30] should look like is more likely to be captured by a disciple of Luis Barragán than Frank Gehry. The significance of LACMA's geographical location within the county[31] should not be overlooked. It is the most prominent public institution in a part of Los Angeles that has served as a focal point for racial desegregation since the 1940s.[32] LACMA needs to be mindful of this history, and especially cautious about committing itself to futuristic architectural statements celebrating the wonders of technology in a neighborhood that is more concerned with human values and traditions.

In the near term, local leaders are not likely to look favorably on any large expenditures for bricks and mortar while programmatic needs go unmet. The key to winning their approval—and, in turn, to gaining their political support—will be to expand the museum's existing educational programs, and to launch new educational initiatives. The potential value of such political support has recently been demonstrated in the context of the state's electricity crisis. Last month, liberals and environmentalists were stunned to see the Mexican American Legal Defense Fund (and the Los Angeles Urban League) weigh in publicly in defense of Southern California Edison and the utility industry in general.[33] These companies have been courting minority groups for years through, inter alia, educational and cultural philanthropy. To the extent that MALDEF and the Urban League are putting their clout in Sacramento behind this position, it might actually turn out to be the deciding factor in whether the utility industry survives in its present form.

In a letter and interview to the Mexican Museum, Alfredo Terrazas, President of the UC Berkeley Alumni Association and Deputy Attorney General for the State of California, offered some instructive thoughts about why museums should become involved in educational programs:

> Research studies and analyses conducted over the past two decades have produced compelling evidence that art studies in the educational curriculum of students help prepare them for the challenges of life and work in our global society. The challenges of today, and most certainly tomorrow, require the abilities, skills, habits, exposure and knowledge that education in the arts is uniquely able to provide.[34]

Terrazas then goes on to offer some creative ideas about how such programs might be structured:

> Why not have students take classes or perform internships at various culturally enriching places like museums?... Perhaps we can structure the immersion experience much like rotating "residencies," an intense two weeks at one museum and then move on. In fact, this would be, by extension, an excellent way to expand cultural exchanges with Mexico and other Latin American countries and to help expose U.C. students to the beautiful cultures in their own backyard.[35]

Judith Huacuja-Pearson at the University of Dayton has also examined new ways of advancing education through the arts under the rubric of service learning.[36] She describes how UD students have become involved with a variety of community-based organizations on projects that have shaped their learning experiences to benefit others as well. Service learning is a concept that appears to be gaining momentum on college and university campuses, and that is also of interest to foundations and corporate donors.[37] LACMA appears to be well positioned to enter this arena, and should consider how the leaders of key constituencies might participate in exploring whether and how such activities could be initiated.

On balance, LACMA is well equipped to manage the challenges it is likely to face in this new century. It has a good collection that has been strengthened immensely by the Lewins's generosity. It has a serviceable, if inelegant, physical plant that adapts well to a wide variety of exhibitions. Unlike an architecturally prominent museum on the opposite coast, it has eschewed the glamour of globalization in favor of cultivating service relationships with its local base of support. It has a management team that has invested wisely and extensively in educational programs and community outreach, presented first-rate exhibitions on a regular basis, and expanded its membership substantially. If it continues on its present course, LACMA should have a bright future in California—regardless of whose California and which California it turns out to be.

Notes

This essay developed out of a graduate seminar led by Professor Bruce Robertson (UC Santa Barbara). I would like to thank him for his useful comments and advice as I was writing and preparing this paper for presentation. He engaged me in lively discussion regarding historical museum practices and the reality of changing demographics and what the future portends.

1. LACMA handout, *Executive Summary*, 9 March 2001, p. 1.

2. The County of Los Angeles, *Annual Report, 2000–2001*, p. 38.

3. LACMA, *Annual Report, 1997/98*, p. 6.

4. Ibid.

5. Ibid., p. 28–31.

6. Stephanie Barron, *Made in California: Art, image, and identity, 1900–2000*, Los Angeles: Los Angeles County Museum of Art; Berkeley: University of California Press, 2000, p. 22.

7. Ibid., p. 27.

8. Ibid., p. 274.

9. Peter Landesman, "A Crisis of Fakes," *New York Times Magazine*, March 18, 2001, p. 77.

10. Christopher Knight, "Taking the Public for a Spin," *Los Angeles Times*, February 16, 2001, p. F-1.

11. Ibid.

12. Ruben Navarrette Jr., "Count Black and White and Brown All Over," *Los Angeles Times*, March 9, 2001, p. B-9.

13. http://planning.co.la.ca.us/rsrch_LACountyProfile.pdf.

14. Aaron Zitner, "Immigrant Tally Doubles in Census," *Los Angeles Times*, March 10, 2001, p. A-1.

15. Alan Nishio, "Race and Education," *UCI Proceedings: A Forum on the President's Initiative on Race, Implications for California*, 1997, Irvine: University of California, Irvine.

16. Antonio Olivio, "3 of 6 Major Mayoral Candidates Skip Forum on the Working Poor," *Los Angeles Times*, March 12, 2001, p. B-3.

17. LACMA, *Annual Report, 1997/98*, p. 47.

18. Patrick J. McDonnell, "Latinos Recover Optimism lost in 90's," *Los Angeles Times*, March 11, 2001, p. B-1.

19. In this respect, it bears a certain resemblance to the University of California, Santa Barbara, which Alfred Moir used to tell his Art History 6C classes was the work of a campus architect named Frank Lloyd Wrong.

20. Suzanne Muchnic, "One LACMA, Undivided?," *Los Angeles Times*, February 23, 2001, p. F-1.

21. In fact, the only major museum that I have visited where I always knew where I was going is the Guggenheim on Fifth Avenue—which is often cited by curators and artists as an example of architectural virtuosity being indulged at the expense of accommodative exhibition space.

22. Suzanne Muchnic, "One LACMA, Undivided?," *Los Angeles Times*, February 23, 2001, p. F-23.

23. Ibid.

24. Ibid.

25. Ibid.

26. Cited in Michael Kimmelman, "The Last Great Art of the 20th Century," *The New York Times*, February 4, 2001, Section 2, p. 39.

27. Tom Carney, "Broad's Way," *Los Angeles Magazine*, February, 1998.

28. Ibid.

29. http://moneycentral.msn.com/investor/invsub/insider/-Details.asp?Pval=2&Symbol=AIG Eli Broad holds 17.21 million shares of American International Group whose stock price has declined from $103 to $73 since December of last year.

30. Miracle Mile.

31. See map—Appendix I.

32. Agustin Gurza, "Haunting Language of Hate in a Property Deed," *Los Angeles Times*, March 20, 2001, p. B-1.

33. John W. Mack, Antonia Hernandez and Angela Oh, "The Utilities Generate a Thousand Points of Light," *Los Angeles Times*, February 22, 2001, p. B-11.

34. Eva Guralnick, "Notes from the Field: Tidal Wave II," *Newsletter of the Mexican Museum*, Fall 2000.

35. Ibid.

36. Judith L. Huacuja-Pearson, "From Sit-Ins to Service Learning," *Newsletter of the College Art Association*, Volume 26, Number 2, March 2001.

37. Christopher Beirn, a personal friend of mine, described to me how Professor Badi Foster championed a highly successful service learning curriculum while he was at Tufts, where he held a chair in political science. There, a model was developed using a civil engineering course on environmental remediation whose students were tasked with applying their newly acquired acknowledge at a polluted site in Roxbury. This involved lots of interaction with community groups, and taught students a great deal about the balance that must be struck between technical know-how and social and political priorities. The project was very popular with students and faculty—especially since it produced an opportunity for the course instructor to publish a paper on civil engineering pedagogy. It also met all the requirements of the national engineering society that accredits such courses. Foster, who has recently been named president of the Phelps Stokes Fund, remains a strong advocate of this concept.

MULTIETHNIC MEXICAN AMERICANS IN DEMOGRAPHIC AND ETHNOGRAPHIC PERSPECTIVES

TOMÁS R. JIMÉNEZ

HARVARD UNIVERSITY

Abstract

This paper examines the ethnic identity of the offspring of Mexican/white intermarriages, or multiethnic Mexican Americans, using both U.S. Census data and 20 in-depth interviews with multiethnic Mexican Americans in California. U.S. Census data on the labels given to children by white/Mexican parent mixes indicate that multiethnic Mexican American children are given a Mexican label much more often than they are given a white non-Hispanic label. These data suggest that the Mexican label will be popular for multiethnic Mexican Americans as they choose identities for themselves. In-depth interviews indicate that respondents claim and assert a Mexican American ethnic identity because it is the most salient ethnicity in their social environment. But as respondents choose their identities, they confront ethnic boundaries, or sharp division between ethnic categories, that influence the extent to which they feel free to assert any one particular identity. They respond to these boundaries by taking a symbolic approach, a Mexican American approach, or a multiethnic approach to their ethnicity. I conclude by discussing the implications of this research for ethnic assimilation of multiethnic Mexican Americans and racial and ethnic inequality.

Introduction

Projections suggest that the Latino[1] population in the United States will grow rapidly (Smith & Edmonston, 1997; Suárez-Orozco, 1998).[2] As this population grows, exogamy rates are high. According to the 1990 United States Census, 28.3 per cent of all married people of Mexican origin were married to a non-Hispanic (U.S. Bureau of the Census, 1998). The choices that children of these intermarriages make about how to identify themselves have implications for how we think about race and ethnicity in the United States (Alonso & Waters, 1993). Traditional notions of race and ethnicity assume that racial and ethnic categories are mutually exclusive. For example, one is either Chinese or Mexican, but not both. Yet multiethnic individuals defy these rigid boundaries.

In this chapter, I examine the identity of multiethnic Mexican Americans—the offspring of intermarriages between one white[3] parent and one Mexican parent—living in California. The relevance is two-fold. First, there is a high prevalence of ethnic intermarriage in California, especially between whites and Latinos, leading to an increase of mixed-ethnic births in California from 12 per cent of all births in 1982 to 14 per cent in 1997. The white/Hispanic mix made up 53 per cent of all mixed-ethnic births in the state in 1997 (Tafoya, 2000). Second, the Western states are home to the largest number of people of Mexican descent in the United States. Fifty-five per cent of all people of Mexican origin in the U.S. lived in the Western region of the United States in 2000 and 25 per cent of all California residents were of Mexican origin in 2000 (U.S. Bureau of the Census, 2001). Perhaps because of the large number of Hispanics in the West, the multiethnic Mexican American population has gone relatively unnoticed in both the academic literature and popular discourse.[4]

This research sheds light on the lives of this population by exploring the content and meaning of ethnic identity of 20 multiethnic Mexican Americans. In what follows, I first situate this research within the existing body of literature on multiethnicity. I then use Census data on the labels that parents of multiethnic Mexican American parents give to their children to indicate some broad trends in the identification of this population. Next, I turn to in-depth interviews that explore the individual ethnic identities of multiethnic Mexican Americans. I conclude by drawing out the theoretical and policy implications of this exploratory study.

Theorizing Multiethnicity

Multiethnicity is conceptualized with reference to the experiences of European ethnic groups. Gordon (1964) argues that structural assimilation, or the entrance of immigrant groups into primary group relationships with the host society, ultimately leads to cultural assimilation, or the taking of a sense of peoplehood from the host culture by the immigrant group (Gordon, 1964, p. 70). Gordon considers intermarriage to be the clearest yardstick of structural assimilation, for under these conditions "the minority group loses its ethnic identity in the larger host or core society, and identificational assimilation takes place" (Gordon, 1964, p. 80).

Gans (1979) argues that large-scale intermarriage among European origin groups has resulted in a symbolic attachment to ethnic identity for later-generation whites, or "a nostalgic allegiance to the culture of the immigrant generation, or that of the old country; a love for and pride in a tradition that can be felt without having to be incorporated in everyday behavior" (Gans, 1979, p. 9). Waters (1990) and Alba (1990) provide empirical evidence of Gans's theory of symbolic ethnicity. Waters (1990) finds that ethnicity is only symbolically felt for white ethnics and that ethnic identity is largely a matter of choice. Similarly, Alba (1990) finds that ethnicity is no longer salient for white ethnics and that intermarriage and the disappearance of large ethnically concentrated communities have reduced ethnic identity to its symbolic form.

It is not clear, however, that non-European immigrant groups—particularly those from Latin American, Asia, and the Caribbean who have arrived since 1965—will follow the same trajectory. The United States is much more racially and ethnically diverse than the monolithic core society outlined in Gordon's work. The identity options available to individuals from post-1965 immigrant ethnic groups are thus varied. Recent theorizing on identity and assimilation points out that these post-1965 immigrant groups may assimilate into many different segments of American society, depending on the extent to which the group experiences discrimination, upward mobility, and the strength of the ethnic enclave (Portes & Zhou, 1993). Individuals from these groups take on the identity of the segment of society into which they assimilate. Recent research shows that assimilation is not a process whereby ethnic groups become more like a single segment of society, but that they may assimilate into one of many segments in a diverse society (Waters, 1994; Waters, 1999).

As intermarriage rates in the United States have dramatically increased in the last forty years, the growing population of multiethnic and multiracial individuals has received increasing research attention. These explorations of multiethnicity depart from the focus on ethnic identity as a dimension of assimilation and focuses on the how multiethnics choose their identities when confronted with mutually exclusive identity choices. Much of this research examines psychological aspects of multiethnicity, focusing on the individual identity choices that multiethnics and multiracials make and argues for the creation of a social space for multiethnic and multiracial individuals (Root, 1992; Root, 1996). Other research focuses on cultural and regional context in which individuals live as variables determining identity choice among multiethnic and multiracial. Multiethnic individuals who live in regions in which there is a large number of multiethnic individuals and thus rich and commonly used vocabulary for identifying persons of multiple ethnic backgrounds are more likely to identify themselves as multiethnic (Stephan & Stephan, 1989). In these regions, multiethnics are accepted as full-fledged members of each of the individual ethnic groups to which they belong, regardless of what those other groups are (Spickard & Fong, 1995; Davis, 1995). In contrast, those who live in regions in which unmixed groups predominate more often choose an unmixed identity because there is no ready-made language for describing their ethnic hybridity (Stephan & Stephan, 1989). Furthermore, the exposure that multiethnics have to a particular aspect of their ethnic identity also influences identity choice. They may feel more attached when they had more cultural exposure to it (i.e., food, holidays, music, lifestyle, and family) and less attached when they have negative experiences with cultural exposure or limited cultural exposure (Stephan, 1991).

Other research has focused on the unique experiences of various multiethnic mixes, showing that the unique combination of ethnic and racial groups to which individuals trace their ethnic backgrounds shapes the experiences and identity choices of these individuals in profound ways (Iijima Hall & Cooke Turner, 2001; Thorton & Gates, 2001).

So too does the combination of racial and ethnic groups to which multiethnic Mexican Americans belong influence how they choose identities. Like European groups, the Mexican-origin population in the United States has experienced high rates of intermarriage with the dominant host group, or "whites." Thus, multiethnic Mexican Americans may be considered evidence of structural assimilation, and, based on the European case, one might predict the emergence of a symbolic form of Mexican ethnicity among this population. However, high rates of European intermarriage took place in the absence of large-scale European immigration, which virtually came to a halt after the Great Depression. In contrast, Mexican immigration and large-scale Mexican/white intermarriage are simultaneous processes. Despite high rates of Mexican intermarriage, Mexican ethnicity remains a vivid part of the United States' racial and ethnic landscape because continued waves of immigration from Mexico refresh it. Mexican clubs, organizations, and neighborhoods are prevalent throughout the U.S., and Mexican cultural customs and practices remain visible and are integral to the daily lives of many people of Mexican descent in the U.S. Thus, multiethnic Mexican Americans choose identities against a social backdrop where part of their ethnic ancestry remains salient.

We know very little about the identities of multiethnic Mexican Americans. How do multiethnic Mexican Americans come to a subjective understanding of their ethnic identity? What are the factors that influence the choices that they make? What are the mechanisms and symbolic forms that multiethnic Mexican Americans use in asserting their ethnic identity? Finally, what implications do these ethnic choices have for the future of Mexican ethnicity among multiethnic Mexican Americans, for racial and ethnic stratification, and for how researchers think about ethnic categories?

Data and Methods

I turn to two sources of data to answer these questions. The first is a 5 per cent sub-sample from the 1990 United States Census Public Use Data Sample consisting of all eligible children from all husband-wife marriages (including unmarried partners) in which one parent is white and the other is identified as Mexican on the Hispanic identification question. In order to ensure that the children are biological offspring of the parents in the sample, families with stepchildren are excluded, as are families in which the number of children in the household is greater than the number born to the mother.

The 1990 Census asked two questions with respect to racial and ethnic identification. The first queries the respondent's race. Among several categories, choices for this question included white, black, and other. A second question asked respondents if they are of Hispanic origin, and respondents are asked to further specify which Hispanic group they are from: Mexican, Puerto Rican, Cuban, and other-Hispanic. I confine my sample to respondents who chose a white, black, or other racial label on the Census form. I have treated the race question and the Hispanic origin question as mutually exclusive, providing a measure of both a person's race and Hispanic origin group. That is, individuals can either be white, white-Mexican, black-Mexican, or other-Mexican. The same range of labels applies to the children in this study.

These data are meant to indicate possible broad trends in the identity of multiethnic Mexican Americans and help to frame the in-depth interviews. The U.S. Census is the only large survey that provides a means for ascertaining which labels are attached to this group. The Census data do not provide a direct measure of how multiethnic Mexican Americans label themselves, but the labels assigned to these individuals by their parents is suggestive of how multiethnic Mexican Americans may label themselves.

Census Data Findings

If the choices that parents make about their children's ethnic label is any indication, the 1990 Census data suggest that multiethnic Mexican Americans choose a Mexican label more than a white label for themselves.

Table 1. Parents' Choice of Children's Identity (All Parents) 1990

Parent Mix	Race and Ethnicity of Children				
	Per cent white	Per cent white-Mexican	Per cent black-Mexican	Per cent other-Mexican	N
white-Mexican/white	41.9	57.81	0	0.29	283,509
black-Mexican/white	19.97	60.36	13.91	5.77	676
other-Mexican/white	30.27	29.64	0.01	40.08	169,817

Source: Calculated from the 1990 United States Census Public Use Data Sample, a 5% sample, selecting for interethnically married parents: one white parent and one Mexican parent.

Table 1 shows that parents of multiethnic Mexican Americans give their children a Mexican label with far greater frequency than they give their children a white label. Although there is variation by the racial label of the parents, no more than 41.9 per cent of children from any parent mix were given a white label. Of all labels given to children, the white-Mexican label is the most common and is particularly popular among children of both white-Mexican/white and black-Mexican/white mixes (57.81 per cent and 60.36 per cent, respectively). This label is also frequently given to children of other-Mexican/white parent mixes (29.64 per cent). The popularity of this label could indicate a reinterpretation of the Census form on the part of the parents. Because the 1990 Census allows parents to choose both a race label and a Hispanic label for their children, it is possible that parents label their children white-Mexican in order to indicate that their children's ethnic lineage can be traced to both a white background and a Mexican background. If multiethnic Mexican Americans follow suit, this pattern suggests that multiethnic Mexican Americans would attempt to label themselves with multiple categories if allowed.

The other-Mexican label is particularly popular for children of other-Mexican/white couples (40.08 per cent).[5] The popularity of the "other" label indicates that multiethnic Mexican Americans may identify with racial and ethnic categories not provided by the Census as a way to indicate that they do not belong completely to either a white or a Mexican category. The use of the "other" may also point to the importance of skin color in choosing labels. This label may communicate that the children have dark skin, and a "white" label may therefore be perceived to be less appropriate than an "other" race label.

Many parents also choose to label their children only white, marking no Hispanic label, despite the fact that they have the option to choose both a racial label and a Hispanic label for their child. The decision not to choose a Hispanic category at all suggests that intermarriage has led some multiethnic Mexican Americans to favor their non-Mexican background, and that Mexican American ethnicity may no longer be a salient part of their ethnic identity.

The Census data suggest broad trends in the ethnic identity of multiethnic Mexican Americans, but there are several short-comings in this data. First, these data only indicate that the labels parents give their children, providing no direct measure of the labels that multiethnic Mexican Americans would choose for themselves. Second, surveys indicate how these individuals may label themselves when they are confined to the labels provided by the Census. Other research has shown that these responses may not indicate a person's actual identity nor the meaning attached to these labels (Waters, 1990). In order to understand how multi-ethnic Mexican Americans identify themselves and the meaning attached to these identities, I turn to analysis of in-depth interviews with these individuals.

In-Depth Interviews

I conducted 20 in-depth interviews[6] with individuals who have one parent who is of a white[7] ethnic origin and one parent who is entirely of Mexican origin, as identified by the respondents. All of the respondents live in Santa Clara County (also known as the Silicon Valley/San José Area). Located in the southern portion of the San Francisco Bay Area, Santa Clara County is a sprawling metropolitan area with a total population of 1,700,976, of which 24 per cent are Hispanic (State of California, Department of Finance, 2000). I chose a single geo-graphic location to ensure respondents negotiate the same general social environment. I also chose Santa Clara County be-cause it closely approximates the California state average for interethnic/interracial births. In 1997, 14 per cent of all births in

California were multiethnic/multiracial, compared to 15 per cent in Santa Clara County in the same year (Tafoya, 2000). Respondents were identified using the snowball sampling technique. After initially interviewing a few respondents, I asked these respondents to recommend others whom I might be able to interview. Most of the people I interviewed fall between the ages of twenty and thirty, and none of the respondents were younger than nineteen or older than forty-one. Interviews lasted between forty-five and 120 minutes, were tape recorded, and transcribed.

Claims made in this section should be treated as testable theoretical assertions and not as generalizable empirical statements. Respondents in my sample are primarily middle class and most are college educated, which may limit the extent to which this research is generalizable to other populations. The middle-class status of my respondents may be an artifact of the very class mobility that often facilitates ethnic intermarriage in the first place (Kalmijn, 1998). However, class and education should be tested as predictors of ethnic attachment among multiethnic Mexican Americans using larger, representative samples, such as the 2000 United States Census.[8]

Checking Boxes, Choosing Identities

I began each in-depth interview by asking the respondent to state how they would identify themselves on forms in which they are asked to check a box denoting their ethnicity, such as a job or school application. Many of the respondents said that they were confused when filling out forms because the given categories often do not match their own specific ethnic background. In light of their confusion, they report a range of responses, most of which they consider to be a compromise.

Simplifying Identities

Consistent with the Census findings, a majority of respondents simplified their ethnicity, identifying themselves as Mexican, Mexican American, or Hispanic. Fourteen of the twenty respondents said that they would check a box that would identify them in this way. There is a range of reasons why respondents choose only one of their ancestries and these reasons offer some explanation for the patterns found in the Census data. Some choose a Mexican/Mexican American/Hispanic label because their non-Mexican ancestry is so mixed that "when it comes to percentages, [the Mexican American background is] the biggest part" (25-year-old male of Mexican and mixed European ancestry). Others who reported themselves as Mexican/Mexican American/Hispanic did so even when they have no "cognitive rule" on which to rely when identifying themselves. Their confusion stems from the fact that the forms usually have no options that would allow them to accurately completely identify their ethnic background.

The reasoning that these respondents give for simplifying their identity on forms points to the importance of ethnic markers in choosing identity categories. Some simplified their identity, claiming only that they are white. One respondent of Mexican and Irish ancestry chose a white identity because he believes that he "looks more Caucasian." Just as parents may have used skin color as a basis for assigning their children's labels on the Census, some children use skin color as a basis for choosing identities on forms, believing that white skin makes them indistinguishable from non-Hispanics whites. Another respondent said that he chose a white label because his father is white and he was told that he should choose his father's identity when he is asked to make a choice. Similarly, one respondent relied on his Spanish surname when choosing an identity category, choosing to simplify his ethnicity to Mexican American because he believed that his Spanish surname identified him as Mexican American.

Choosing the "Other" or Choosing Them All

Census data showed that the "other" label and "white-Mexican" label were particularly prevalent choices for parents of multiethnic Mexican Americans, suggesting that these labels may also be popular for multiethnic Mexican Americans as they choose their own identities. Consistent with the Census data, many respondents said that they would choose "other" or that they would check all of the boxes that represent their ethnic background because they were dissatisfied with the available categories, which do not seem to depict how they identify themselves. The comments of a 26-year-old female of Mexican and Irish ancestry typify the sentiments of these respondents:

Like, if it only says check one, I pick "other" because there isn't one that says Mexican and Irish or Mexican American. It's always Hispanic. Or they have [a] million different terms for Mexican and then black or whatever. But there's never one that says half this and half that.

These responses support the hypothesis that the "other-Mexican" and "white-Mexican" labels were associated with multiethnic Mexican Americans with great frequency because there were no available categories that accurately described their background. By choosing "other" or checking multiple boxes (i.e., white *and* Mexican), multiethnic Mexican Americans attempt to manipulate the mutually exclusive categories in order to more accurately represent their ethnic background.

Choosing Identities in Daily Life: The Salience of Mexican American Ethnicity

Just as respondents must make choices when completing forms, they must also select from readily available identities in interactive settings, which are in turn influenced by the availability and salience of particular ethnic identities. As the Census data suggests, multiethnic Mexican Americans gravitate toward a Mexican American ethnic identity more than they do a white identity as they choose identities in their daily lives. Of the available ethnicities, Mexican American ethnicity is perhaps the most salient because of their geographic location and the recent and continuous flow of immigration from Mexico. The strong presence of Mexican Americans and continual influx of Mexican immigrants maintain and refresh Mexican culture, customs, and practices in California. These factors make Mexican American ethnicity a more available ethnic option. As a twenty four-year-old woman of Mexican and Canadian descent put it,

[L]iving here where I do, and it's really a Mexican-like [city]. This town has a lot of Mexican culture surrounding it, and you don't see shops flying Canadian flags, y'know. I've just had a lot more contact with my Mexican culture.

Respondents also mentioned more specific avenues through which a Mexican American ethnicity is made available to them and as an ethnic identity choice: schooling, travel, and family.

Schooling

High school and college facilitate exposure to Mexican and Mexican American ethnicity both formally and informally. Formally, schools support Mexican and Mexican American cultural customs through courses offered on Mexican American history and culture, school-sponsored clubs and organizations, and school-sponsored celebration of holidays (i.e., *Cinco de Mayo*). Informally, schools facilitate exposure to Mexican ethnicity by providing a place where multiethnic Mexican Americans form friendships and social networks with Mexicans and Mexican Americans, as a number of respondents reported that Mexican and Mexican American peers and dating partners in both high school and college led them to identify more strongly with their Mexican American background.

Travel

Travel to Mexico also provides a means through which respondents are exposed to their Mexican origins, lending further strength to their preference for a Mexican American identity. The close proximity of Mexico to the United States makes travel to Mexico relatively easy. A number of respondents had taken trips to Mexico to study, for vacation, or to visit family.

Family

The family plays a key role in the extent to which Mexican American ethnicity is reinforced in the respondents' lives. Respondents who had large and close knit families—both immediate and extended—tended to gravitate toward their Mexican American ethnicity more than respondents who did not. They reported that their frequent interaction with Mexican American extended family members gave them a sense of family history and exposure to aspects of Mexican and Mexican American customs and culture. Other respondents mentioned that the quality of interactions with their Mexican American side of their family—as compared to their non-Mexican American side of the family—influenced their sense of ethnic identity. They noted that gatherings and interactions with their non-Mexican side of the family tended to focus on events that were devoid of ethnic themes, and conversations with these family members revolved around their daily lives, apart from ethnicity. In contrast, gatherings and interactions with their Mexican American side of the family reflected Mexican American themes in the form of language, food, and family history.

The Role of Symbolic Ethnicity

The extent to which a Mexican American ethnicity was an option must also be considered in comparison to the relative salience of the alternatives. Nearly all of the respondents reported having very little knowledge of and minimal exposure to their non-Mexican American ethnic background. Their "other" background was too detached from the ethnic homeland (i.e., too many generations removed from the immigrant generation) to permit any strong attachment or knowledge of those points of origin. If their non-Mexican side was a melange of European ethnicities, no single alternative emerged. Many of their non-Mexican American background was simply too "mixed-up" to amount to a salient counterpart. Furthermore, the low visibility of their white ethnic background in their social environment contributed to their weak attachment to this aspect of their ethnic background. The lack of ethnic specific structures—neighborhoods, celebrations, political movements, etc.—in Santa Clara County and California created few opportunities for multiethnic Mexican Americans to experience their non-Mexican background in any meaningful way.

Between minimal exposure to their non-Mexican American lineage and considerable exposure to their Mexican background, the latter becomes more available, accessible, and meaningful to respondents as they choose their ethnic identity on forms and in daily life.

Negotiating Ethnic Boundaries

The Census data and the interview data reported thus far indicate a stronger attachment to Mexican American ethnicity for multiethnic Mexican Americans relative to other identity choices. But analysis of interview data on how multiethnic Mexican Americans assert their ethnic identity indicate that sharp boundaries between ethnic categories complicate respondents' identity choices in their daily lives. They report numerous experiences in which they must negotiate boundaries between ethnic categories and the difficulty that they have crossing back and forth between them. It is through this process of negotiation that the respondents choose, assert, and sometimes lose a particular identity.

Ethnic Boundaries and the Family

Ethnic boundaries surface within their own families. Respondents noted being made fun of by extended family members because they lack characteristics that are often associated with being of Mexican descent, such as dark skin and the ability to speak Spanish. In some cases, parents or extended family members strongly encouraged or pressured respondents to place more importance on a particular component of their ethnic background to the exclusion of another.

The boundaries between ethnic categories were especially clear for those respondents whose parents are divorced. The differences between their parents' backgrounds are often accentuated because they are used as a basis for disputes between the parents. Living in a divorced family led some respondents to see their ethnic backgrounds as compartmentalized, mutually exclusive components of their family's ethnic lineage.

Confronting Prejudice

These choices do not take place against a neutral backdrop. Prejudice directed at people of Mexican descent is a feature of everyday life, but one that only indirectly impacts the children of these mixed marriages. Because most of the respondents can pass as white, they are often exposed to the world of white racism and hear comments that many darker skinned people of Mexican descent may not hear. A twenty-four-year-old woman of Mexican and Canadian background recalled the reactions that her high school friends had to Mexican immigrants who frequented the same shopping mall:

> [I]f [the Mexican immigrants] looked at any of my friends, they would just start telling them to "fuck off" and "What are you looking at?"... And that was hard for us too, because it was like, what do you say?... [I]f they weren't a really close friend and they didn't know my background, and just from the way I looked they would just assume that

I was totally white. And I would have this going on inside me, like feeling like kinda' sick to my stomach, feeling anxious, like what do I say, y'know?... Especially when it's about you and your family, y'know. And I'm like, my family looks like the people they're making fun of, y'know?

Confrontations with racism remind respondents of their simultaneous connection to multiple ethnic categories. Their white skin is not normally associated with American conceptions of what people of Mexican descent look like and their experience as a "white" person allows them an insider's view of white racism. When they are confronted with racism, they are also reminded of the sharp divisions that exist between their multiple ethnic backgrounds.

Affirmative Action

Ethnic identity carries material rewards in an era of affirmative action programs in colleges and employment. Some respondents felt that they did not deserve to benefit from affirmative action despite the fact that they qualify. Some refused to mark Mexican American categories when filling out applications because they believed that their privileged background and white skin precluded them from reaping the benefits of affirmative action that come with marking such categories.

Since a valuable resource is at stake, ethnicity becomes a gatekeeper and "purer" bearers of Mexican American identity were willing to slam the door on their multiethnic cousins. For example, one respondent joined a high school program designed to help high-achieving minority students enter college, but felt that he was not accepted by the other students, and particularly by Mexican American students:

[E]verybody in the club was looking at me weird. Like I didn't belong there...This Mexican girl, she was like, "What are you in here for? No, no you couldn't be [Mexican American]." And so I left. I never went back. (29-year-old Mexican and Irish male)

Choosing a Mexican American box on forms means claiming membership to an underrepresented and historically disadvantaged group.[9] Many perceive that they have not experienced the same discrimination that poorer or darker-skinned people of

Mexican descent have encountered (Telles & Murguía, 1990; Murguía & Telles, 1996). Their beliefs are confirmed when respondents run into "purer" Mexican Americans who remind respondents that they do not have the "right" biography to be considered a minority.

Other respondents did not experience this same dilemma and were quite willing to claim a Mexican American identity in order to benefit from affirmative action policies. For example, a 26-year-old woman of Mexican and Irish descent unabashedly claimed:

> I used to play the Mexican side a little bit, you know, when affirmative action was (pause)…(laugh) I'll take anything, I'm not proud.
>
> Q: Tell me about that.
>
> R: When it's obvious that they don't want a white girl or they are trying to make their quota or whatever it is, yeah, forget the Irish (laugh).

For these respondents, multiethnicity permits the claiming of benefits that accrue to a Mexican American identity without having to experience the discrimination that many people of Mexican descent often run into. They do not see their opportunistic use of ethnicity as making any strong claims about their own ethnic identity. Rather, they view themselves as simply benefiting in an instrumental way from that for which they legally qualify.

Authenticity Tests

Peers, clubs, and organizations are a primary means through which Mexican American ethnicity is ratified among multiethnic Mexican Americans. Yet just as these opportunities reinforce the Mexican American ethnicity, they are also a means of exclusion. Respondents often run into boundaries between ethnic categories due to their mixed ethnic background and lack of ability to openly display Mexican American ethnicity, such as having dark skin, having a Spanish surname, being able to speak Spanish, and knowledge of Mexican and Mexican American culture.

Clubs or organizations that celebrate Mexican and Mexican American ethnicity—such as MEChA[10]—either in high school or in college are important sites of ethnic articulation. But membership does not necessarily signal acceptance for multiethnic Mexican Americans who were often rejected by the members or made to feel as an outsider at club gatherings. As with having white skin, not being able to speak Spanish limits the extent to which respondents are seen as authentically Mexican American. Although many "purer" Mexican Americans do not speak Spanish, these multiethnic respondents believed that their own lack of ability to speak Spanish is another reason why they feel unwelcome in Mexican American clubs and organizations. Whether experienced or expected, rejection from people of Mexican descent upon joining clubs and organizations deters many respondents from asserting a Mexican identity altogether.

The ethnic boundaries that respondents encounter are also self-imposed, as many questioned their own right to assert a Mexican identity. For example, a 27-year-old Mexican, Polish, and Russian man who once danced *balet folklorico*, the folk dances of Mexico, said that he felt hypocritical for performing these dances. When asked why, he explained, "[I]t's partly because I tell myself that I'm not really—I'm not full Mexican so I don't have the right to [participate]." Participating in Mexican and Mexican American cultural customs or joining clubs and organizations means staking claim to a Mexican American identity that respondents themselves perceive to be only partially authentic.[11]

Multiethnic Mexican Americans and the Ethnic Narrative

Cornell (2000) argues that ethnicity can be understood as a form of narrative. Groups of individuals select, plot, and interpret events that are common to their experiences. The result of this process is the construction of a narrative that "captures the central understanding of what it means to be a member of [a] group" (Cornell, 2000, p. 42). As Cornell points out, narratives help ethnic groups distinguish between "us" and "them."

While the content and boundaries of a particular ethnic narrative are continually contested and negotiated, the Mexican experience in the U.S. is defined by a number of key conditions:

conquest, immigration, poverty, discrimination, protest, and struggle. Multiethnic Mexican Americans in this study respond to these core conditions and events as they consider their own ethnic identity, but in ways that highlight their ambivalence.

Their own biographies depart from the Mexican American narrative. "I could appreciate [the Mexican American's] struggle from afar, but I didn't live it," one man told me. Respondents perceive these differences most keenly when "purer" Mexican Americans reject them because they do not possess the surface traits and characteristics that are often associated with people of Mexican descent: dark skin color, ability to speak Spanish, knowledge of Mexican and Mexican American culture, surnames, blood-line and the like. The dilemma that some respondents face with affirmative action best illustrates this point. Affirmative action policies are generally designed to offset the effects of discrimination on those groups that have experienced historic and present-day discrimination. Affirmative action policies reinforce discrimination as a central aspect of the Mexican American narrative because anyone who is of Mexican descent qualifies for affirmative action. As multiethnic Mexican Americans choose their identity on forms or in their daily lives, they must consider the extent to which they have experienced racial or ethnic discrimination on the basis of their ethnic background.

Often times it is other Mexican Americans who police the extent to which multiethnic Mexican Americans may claim membership in a Mexican American narrative. Recall the respondent whose right to be in a school program for high achieving minority students was questioned by the other members. His right to be in the organization was questioned because his biography—his narrative—was perceived to be different than that which is necessary to qualify for the program. This incident forced him to consider the extent to which his experiences interact with the events at the core of the Mexican American narrative. As is the case with many multiethnic Mexican Americans, he concluded that his experiences as a middle class individual with white skin preclude him from membership in the Mexican American narrative. However, claiming one's membership is far less taxing when there is no Mexican American audience to rebuff claims of membership to a Mexican American narrative, as in the case of the respondents who use their Mexican American backgrounds solely to benefit from affirmative action.

The experience of confronting prejudice also forces respondents to consider their connection to the Mexican American narrative. Respondents can pass as white, allowing their peers to feel comfortable enough to make prejudicial comments. They escape the very burdens that affirmative action is meant to remedy and reinforce the way in which their own experience departs from the legacy of discrimination that many "real" Mexican Americans know too well. On the other hand, hearing prejudicial comments strikes a chord with some respondents, as they recognize that such comments are an affront to their Mexican American family members and ancestors. Thus, respondents cannot entirely ignore their connection to being a Mexican American.

It is through experiences such as these that respondents come to feel more like one of "them" than one of "us." If, as Cornell (2000) argues, ethnic categories are categories of collective stories that define what it means to be a member of a particular ethnic group, there is no widely recognized ethnic category or label that depicts the set of experiences that is the multiethnic Mexican American's narrative.

Negotiating Ethnic Boundaries: Approaches to Ethnic Identity

The in-depth interviews revealed that multiethnic Mexican Americans take three approaches to their ethnic identity: a symbolic identity, a Mexican American identity, and a multiethnic identity.[12] It is important to note that many respondents report identities that fit one or more of these types of identities, as ethnic identity varied depending on the situation in which respondents found themselves.

Symbolic Identity

Many of the respondents describe their attachment as that of "a nostalgic allegiance to the culture of the immigrant generation, or that of the old country; a love for and pride in a tradition that can be felt without having to be incorporated in everyday behavior" (Gans, 1979, p. 9). For some, a symbolic identity stems from their limited experience with and knowledge of their ethnic roots. These respondents primarily experience their Mexican American ethnicity through ethnic cuisine and celebrating certain ethnic holidays. For example, some respondents mentioned eating tamales during the holidays as a primary means through which they experience their Mexican American heritage.

Other respondents described the enjoyment that they received from being of Mexican descent because it allows them to be something other than "just white." As Waters (1990, chapter 7) points out, asserting a symbolic identity allows individuals to assert themselves as an individual, or as this respondent put it, her Mexican American background gives her "flavor." Yet, symbolic ethnicity also allows respondents to be part of a larger collective above and beyond a particular ethnic group; a collective for which ethnicity is not at its core.

By asserting a symbolic ethnic identity, respondents do not push or cross ethnic boundaries, and therefore mitigate the extent to which they must negotiate such boundaries. In so doing, respondents avoid potential rejection that they experience when claiming a Mexican American identity, yet they maintain some connection—albeit symbolic—to their Mexican American heritage.

Mexican American Identity

A second approach to ethnic identity that respondents take is characterized by a strong affinity for Mexican American ethnicity. The respondents who take on a Mexican American identity see themselves as Mexican American and assert a Mexican American ethnicity. These multiethnic Mexican Americans actively seek out Mexican and Mexican American cultural celebrations, clubs, and organizations, participate in Mexican traditions, and are politically active in causes and movements related to Mexican American ethnicity.

Despite the fact that some of these respondents reported running into rejection born out of boundary maintenance, they persisted in asserting a Mexican identity, asserting "I'm Mexican too!" Why would some respondents persist in asserting a Mexican American identity at the risk of being rejected or stigmatized? Two structural changes provide potential explanations. First, there have been significant changes in the socio-political structure for California Mexican Americans in the last thirty years. The post Civil Rights culture in California allows and often encourages individuals to maintain a connection to their ethnic roots, as a number of ethnic holidays are recognized in school and in civic celebrations. Furthermore, Mexican Americans occupy a number of local and state positions of political power in California, contributing to the positive visibility of California Mexican Americans. Thus, many respondents see a Mexican American identity as a positive ethnic option.

A second factor has to do with demographic changes. A majority of the residents in Santa Clara County are non-white. Therefore, asserting a Mexican American identity means claiming membership to the majority group in Santa Clara County. It may be the case that respondents persist in choosing a Mexican American identity because they would rather be a part of the (numerical) majority. I can only speculate on how these structural changes influence identity choices from the given data. However, this line of research deserves further empirical investigation and theoretical development.

The "Third Way"

A third approach to ethnic identity is the multiethnic approach. In formulating his argument about ethnicity as a narrative, Cornell (2000) points out that there is an emerging multiethnic narrative that is characterized by a common experience of not fitting the established categories. The narratives "are narratives of connection, focused not on the boundaries—on what separates people—but on connection, on the intertwined patterns of descent that muddy boundaries, fuzz differences, and create shared narrative space" (Cornell, 2000, p. 50). The comments of many respondents are exemplary of the multiethnic narrative that Cornell describes. Some respondents described a rejection of the available official ethnic identities, as those narratives do not accurately depict their own experience. Recall that others took a multiethnic approach in choosing their ethnic identity when filling out forms, choosing to identify multiple categories or choose "other" so as not be placed entirely in one category when filling out forms. In so doing, respondents assert their affirmative connection to multiple ethnic narratives.

For some, the multiethnic narrative is one that respondents "fall back on" in response to not feeling entirely Mexican

American. In describing her peer group in high school, a twenty-four-year-old woman of Mexican and Danish descent noted that she never felt entirely comfortable spending time with students who were completely of Mexican descent. Instead, she chose to spend time with other multiethnic students, some of whom were also multiethnic Mexican Americans.

For others, the multiethnic identity is an increasingly recognized, primary identity. Many respondents prefer to think of themselves a simultaneously fitting into a number of ethnic categories and as being part of a number of ethnic narratives:

> [M]ost people tend to want to make me only white or only Mexican. And I'm like, that's not who I am. You have to take in all of me. (twenty-four-year-old Mexican and Canadian woman)

Others conveyed their simultaneous connection to multiple backgrounds by displaying flags, posters, or artwork representing each of their backgrounds. Just as the large presence of Mexican American peers have influenced a number of respondents to become more aware of their Mexican American identity, the growing number of multiethnic individuals led some respondents to become more aware of an emerging multiethnic narrative.

Discussion and Conclusion

This exploratory research shows that multiethnic Mexican Americans encounter ethnic boundaries in many aspects of their lives. Census data on the labels that parents of multiethnic Mexican Americans give to their children suggest that multiethnic Mexican Americans on aggregate may gravitate toward their Mexican ethnic heritage. The findings in the Census data mirror findings from in-depth interviews. When filling out forms, most respondents simplify their ethnicity, calling themselves Mexican, Mexican American, or Hispanic. Still others choose to mark more than one box or refer to their background simply as "other." The people I interviewed believe that the responses that they give are generally a compromise because no category accurately describes their own background. The dilemmas that they experience when filling out forms arc similar to those that they experience as they choose identities in their daily lives. Multiethnic Mexican Americans must choose from ethnic identities that are readily available. Mexican American ethnicity narrative is especially available in their social environment because of the strong presence of people of Mexican descent who live in California and in Santa Clara County. Because some part of their own ethnic lineage can be traced to a Mexican narrative, multiethnic Mexican Americans confront boundaries that exist between their own multiethnic narrative and prevailing narratives of the Mexican population in the United States. Multiethnic Mexican Americans respond to confrontations these boundaries with one or more approaches to their ethnic identity: a symbolic approach, a Mexican American approach, or a multiethnic approach. This research has several implications for theorizing on ethnicity and policy.

The Future of Ethnic Identity for Multiethnic Mexican Americans

I began this paper by pointing out that multiethnic Mexican Americans present an interesting case of Gordon's (1964) theory of assimilation. While this population is structurally assimilated because they are products of intermarriage, they negotiate an environment in which Mexican American ethnicity remains salient. The Census data presented suggests that despite their mixed ethnic background, multiethnic Mexican Americans may maintain a strong attachment to a Mexican American identity. However, interview data reveals that their identity choices are complicated by their mixed heritage in ways that the Census data do not reveal. Furthermore, the interview data indicate that being children of intermarriage may not mean assimilating into a monolithic core society, as Gordon's theory would predict. What exactly will assimilation entail for this group? In California, the "core society" is anything but monolithic with respect to ethnicity. California is home to more immigrants than any other state and has a large number of multiethnic individuals. Therefore, determining what assimilation means for multiethnic Mexican Americans requires taking stock of the ethnic identities that are available in the social contexts that multiethnic Mexican Americans negotiate.

If the prevailing established categories—white and Mexican American—remain the only that are available, then multiethnic Mexican Americans may continue to choose their ethnic identity in reference to these two categories, asserting themselves as members of one of the narratives that one of these categories represent.

Alternatively, multiethnic Mexican Americans may have another option: a multiethnic identity. As intermarriage rates continue to climb, a critical mass of people who do not fit into the traditional categories of race and ethnicity will grow. This critical mass may bring forth the emergence of a new narrative— the multiethnic narrative. There is evidence of the emergence of a multiethnic narrative, and this multiethnic narrative is gaining legitimacy within the larger society. In popular culture, a number of celebrities have begun to openly claim a "mixed," or multiethnic identity. Similarly, a number of student-clubs and organizations that celebrate multiethnicity have emerged on college and university campuses across the United States. Perhaps the greatest evidence of the emergence of a multiethnic narrative can be found in the institutionalization of this ethnic identity. The Executive Office of Management and Budget (OMB) Statistical Directive No. 15, which "provides standard for classification for record keeping, collection and presentation of data on race and ethnicity in Federal program administrative reporting and statistical activities" (OMB Directive No. 15, in Root, 1996), now allows for respondents to check more than one racial category when filling out federal forms, such as the 2000 U.S. Census. Combined, a critical mass of multiethnic individuals, celebrities who promote their multiethnicity, clubs and organizations, and OMB Statistical Directive No. 15 help to give the multiethnic narrative some currency with the larger society.

Ethnic Options and Social Consequences

Multiethnic Mexican Americans have ethnic options (Waters, 1990). They can choose to invoke a particular ethnicity when they so desire, but otherwise negotiate their social environment without being recognized as distinctly "ethnic." But unlike white ethnics, the consequences, both positive and negative, attached to their ethnic options are significant. As a number of the respondents note, invoking a Mexican American identity carries significant material benefits, especially where affirmative action is concerned.

On the other hand, invoking a Mexican identity can have negative consequences. Mexican Americans are a socially stigmatized group and are often the victims of prejudice and discrimination. Invoking a particular Mexican American identity or cultural stance may open up respondents to the injuries of prejudice and discrimination, even if respondents can pass as white. The stakes can be high when choosing a particular identity, as the costs and benefits associated with identity choices may have a significant influence on respondents' economic and social outcomes.

The costs and benefits of these identity choices have implications for how we understand the place of multiethnic Mexican Americans in the context of racial and ethnic stratification. As this research points out, multiethnics are a group of people with a unique narrative—one that does not simply fall somewhere in between a minority and a white narrative. Yet under the current system of categorization, multiethnics are absorbed into mutually exclusive categories. Given their experiences, what is unclear is whether or not multiethnics ought to be considered members of a disadvantaged group, or something else altogether. That is, as we decide who the "truly disadvantaged" are, how will multiethnics be viewed? Are multiethnics members of disadvantaged groups? Should multiethnics benefit from affirmative action? As policy makers and society in general look to understand racial and ethnic stratification and change, these questions are some of the many with which we will be faced.

Notes

1. "Hispanic" or "Latino" refers to person of Mexican, Puerto Rican, Cuban, Central/South American, Dominican, or Spanish descent.

2. Suárez-Orozco (1998) uses United States Census data to show that by the year 2050, Latinos will make up 24.5 per cent of the total U.S. population.

3. I use the term "white" to refer to people who are white *and* non-Hispanic.

4. See Johnson (1999) for an autobiographical sketch of the multiethnic Mexican American experience.

5. Calculations of the labels given to children by race/ethnicity and gender of parent reveal similar findings. Consistent with the findings in Table 1, children are given a Mexican label far more often than they are given a white label, regardless of the mother's or father's label. These calculations are available upon request from the author.

6. A copy of the interview protocol is available upon request from the author.

7. Recall that I use the term "white" to refer to people who are white *and* non-Hispanic.

8. Individual-level data samples from the 2000 U.S. Census were not available for public use at the time of this writing.

9. Mexican Americans are considered underrepresented and historically disadvantaged under federal and some state affirmative action policies.

10. MEChA is a student organization, which stands for *movimiento estudiantil Chicano de Aztlán*, or Chicano student movement of *Aztlán*. MEChA was founded during the Chicano movement of the 1960s and 1970s and has chapters on high school and college campuses throughout the United States.

11. Despite the fact that they are mostly middle class and college educated, the respondents did not mention their class status as a reason for their authenticity being challenged. Research on middle class African Americans has shown that class status is seen as a challenge to middle class their African American ethnic authenticity (Lacy, 2000). However, similar evidence did not emerge from my in-depth interviews. One possible explanation is that Mexicans Americans of *equal* class and educational status, such as college classmates, challenged the respondents' ethnic authenticity. Thus, class did not emerge as a basis for such challenges.

12. For an extensive discussion of the various approaches to multiethnicity among multiethnics and multiracials, see Nakashima (1996).

References

Alba, R., & Nee, V. (1997). Rethinking assimilation theory for a new era of immigration. *The International Migration Review*, 31(4), 826–874.

Alba, R. D. (1985). *Italian Americans: Into the twilight of ethnicity*. Englewood Cliffs, N.J.: Prentice-Hall.

_____. (1990). *Ethnic identity: The transformation of white America*. New Haven: Yale University Press.

Alonso, W., & Waters, M. (1993). *The future composition of the American population: An illustrative projection*. Paper presented at the Winter Meetings of the American Statistical Association, Fort Lauderdale, Florida.

Changing face of the future: Mixed-race births could make old divisions obsolete. (1999, April 18). *San Jose Mercury News*, pp. A1, A22.

Cornell, S. (2000). That's the story of our life. In P. R. Spickard & W. J. Burroughs (Eds.), *Narrative and Multiplicity in Constructing Ethnic Identities* (pp. 41–53). Philadelphia: Temple University Press.

Davis, J. (1995). The Hawaiian alternative to the one-drop rule. In N. Zack (Ed.), *American mixed race: The culture of microdiversity* (pp. 115–131). Lanham: Rowan and Littlefield Publishers.

Department of Finance, State of California. (2000). *Race/ethnic population estimates: Components of change for California counties*, March 12, 2000, from http://www.dof.ca.gov/html/Demograp/Race-eth.htm.

Executive Office of Management and Budget. (1996). Statistical directive 15. In M. P. P. Root (Ed.), *The multiracial experience: Racial borders as the new frontier* (pp. 411–411–414). Thousand Oaks: Sage Publications.

Frankenberg, R. (1993). *White women, race matters: The social construction of whiteness.* Minneapolis: University of Minnesota Press.

Gans, H. J. (1979). Symbolic ethnicity: The future of ethnic groups and cultures in America. *Ethnic and Racial Studies*, 2(January), 1–20.

Gordon, M. M. (1964). *Assimilation in American life: The role of race, religion, and national origins.* New York: Oxford University Press.

Iijima Hall, C., & Cooke Turner, T. (2001). The diversity of biracial individuals: Asian-white and Asian-minority biracial identity. In T. Williams-León & C. L. Nakashima (Eds.), *The sum of our parts: Mixed heritage Asian Americans* (pp. 81–91). Philadelphia: Temple University Press.

Johnson, K. R. (1998). *How did you get to be Mexican?: A white/brown man's search for identity.* Philadelphia: Temple University Press.

Kalmijn, M. (1998). Intermarriage and homogamy: Causes, patterns, and trends. *Annual Review of Sociology*, 24, 395–421.

Lacy, K. (2000). *Negotiating black identities: The construction and use of social boundaries among middle-class black suburbanites.* Cambridge: Harvard University.

Murguía, E., & Telles, E. (1996). Phenotype and schooling among Mexican Americans. *Sociology of Education*, 69(October), 276–289.

Nakashima, C. L. (1996). Voices from the movement: Approaches to multiraciality. In M. P. P. Root (Ed.), *The multiracial experience: Racial borders as the new frontier* (pp. 79–97). Thousand Oaks: Sage Publications.

Portes, A., & Zhou, M. (1993). The new second generation: Segmented assimilation and its variants. *Annals of the American Academy of Political and Social Science*, 530(November), 74–96.

Root, M. P. P. (1992). *Racially mixed people in America.* Newbury Park, CA: Sage.

Root, M. P. P. (1996). *The multiracial experience: Racial borders as the new frontier.* Thousand Oaks, CA: Sage.

Smith, JP & Edmonston, B. (1997). *The new Americans: Economic, demographic and fiscal impact of immigration.* Washington, DC: National Academy Press.

Spickard, P. R., & Fong, R. (1995). Pacific Islander Americans and multiethnicity: A vision of America's future? *Social Forces*, 73(4), 1365–1383.

Stephan, C. W. (1991). Ethnic identity among mixed-heritage people in Hawaii. *Symbolic Interaction*, 14(3), 261–277.

Stephan, C. W., & Stephan, W. (1989). After intermarriage: Ethnic identity among mixed heritage Japanese-Americans and Hispanics. *Journal of Marriage and the Family*, 51(May), 507–519.

Suárez-Orozco, M. M. (1998). Introduction. In C. Suárez-Orozco (Ed.), *Crossings: Mexican immigration in interdisciplinary perspectives.* Cambridge: David Rockefeller Center/Harvard University Press.

Tafoya, S. M. (2000). *Check one or more … mixed race and ethnicity.* San Francisco: California Public Policy Institute.

Telles, E., & Murguía, E. (1990). Phenotype discrimination and income differences among Mexican Americans. *Social Science Quarterly*, 71(4), 682–696.

Thorton, M., & Gates, H. (2001). Black, Japanese, and American: An Asian American identity yesterday and today. In T. Williams-León & C. L. Nakashima (Eds.), *The sum of our parts: Mixed heritage Asian Americans.* Philadelphia: Temple University Press.

United States Census Bureau. (1998). Interracial tables calculated from the 1990 Census of Population and Housing, Public Use Microdata Samples. Retrieved November 16, 1999, from the World Wide Web: http://www.census.gov/population/socdemo/race/interractab3.txt.

_____ (2000). The Hispanic population in the United States, March 1999: Population Characteristics. Retrieved March 8, 2000 from the World Wide Web: http://www.census.gov/prod/2000pubs/p20-527.pdf.

_____. (2001). U.S. Census 2000 redistricting data. Retrieved June 16, 2001 from the World Wide Web:http://factfinder.census.gov/bf/_lang=en_vt_name=DEC_2000_PL_U_QTPL_geo_id=04000US06.html.

_____. (2001). The Hispanic population: 2000 US Census brief. Retrieved June 16, 2001 from the World Wide Web: http://www.census.gov/prod/2001pubs/c2kbr01-3.pdf.

Waters, M. C. (1990). *Ethnic options: Choosing identities in America.* Berkeley: University of California Press.

_____. (1999). *Black identities: West Indian immigrant dreams and American realities.* Cambridge: Russell Sage Foundation, Harvard University Press.

_____. (1994). Ethnic and racial identities of second generation black immigrants in New York City. *International Migration Review*, 28, 795–820.

CONTRIBUTORS

MARC CORONADO is a painter, a gardener, and mother of Demetrius Lambrinos. She is a Ph.D. candidate in English at the University of California, Santa Barbara, and teaches literature, composition and critical thinking, and Ethnic Studies at UCSB and Santa Barbara City College. Her dissertation is a look at the rhetoric of Multiracial Studies.

CARINA EVANS is a graduate student at the University of California, Santa Barbara, where she studies twentieth-century American literature. Her particular interest lies in the intersection between race and gender, encompassing both literature and popular culture. Recent work includes writing on biracial identity across history, with special attention paid to novels by William Faulkner, Nella Larsen, and Danzy Senna.

MELINDA GÁNDARA is currently a graduate student in the History of Art and Architecture at the University of California, Santa Barbara. She works in the field of Latin American art and is interested in museum practices. She is a strong advocate for equity in education and has written articles on university outreach.

RUDY P. GUEVARRA, JR. is of Mexican and Filipino heritage. He is a doctoral student in American History at the University of California, Santa Barbara, where he also earned his M.A. degree. He holds a B.A. degree in History with minors in Ethnic Studies and Philosophy from the University of San Diego. His research interests include twentieth century U.S. labor history, Chicano history, Asian Pacific American history, race and ethnicity, and multiethnic/multiracial identity. His dissertation-in-progress is a comparative social history of Mexicans and Filipinos in San Diego, as well as an analysis of Mexipino multiethnic identity.

TOMAS JIMÉNEZ is a Ph.D. candidate in the department of sociology at Harvard University. His research focuses on immigration, immigrant-group adaptation processes, ethnic identity, and inequality. At present, Jimenez is working on an ethnographic exploration of the relationship between Mexican immigrants and American-born Mexicans in a small midwestern town and a small western city. He is also working on a paper with Mary C. Waters that highlights the latest research on the immigrant experience and maps out an agenda for future research. The paper will appear in the 2003 edition of the *Annual Review of Sociology*.

GEORGE LIPSITZ is Professor of Ethnic Studies at the University of California, San Diego, where he directs the Thurgood Marshall Institute and the San Diego Social Science History Project. His publications include *American Studies in a Moment of Danger* (2001), *The Possessive Investment in Whiteness* (1998), *A Life in the Struggle: Ivory Perry and the Culture of Opposition, Rainbow at Midnight* (1994), *Dangerous Crossroads* (1994), *Sidewalks of St. Louis* (1991), and *Time Passages* (1990).

JEFFREY MONIZ graduated from Beloit College in Wisconsin, earning a B.A. in History and a Master of Arts in Teaching degree in Elementary Education. He recently earned another M.A. and is a Ph.D. candidate in the Cultural Perspectives in Education Emphasis at UCSB. He has taught elementary and middle grades in such diverse settings as inner city Leeds, England; urban and suburban Beloit, Wisconsin; downtown Honolulu, and rural Molokai, Hawai'i. He teaches Crosscultural Education for the Teacher Education Program at UCSB. Born and raised in Hawai'i, Jeff is of Ilocano (Filipino), Azorean (Portuguese), and Chinese descent.

PAUL SPICKARD is the father of Naomi Spickard and Daniel Spickard. He teaches history, Asian American studies, and multiracial studies at the University of California, Santa Barbara. He has written ten books on race in America and related subjects, and is currently working on a novel.

LAURA FURLAN SZANTO (Apache/Osage/Cherokee) is a doctoral student in English at the University of California, Santa Barbara, specializing in American Indian literatures. She received a B.A. in American Studies from the University of Iowa and an M.A. in English from San Diego State. Laura's work on Louise Erdrich has appeared in *Studies in American Indian Literatures*. Her dissertation examines representations of urban Indians in contemporary fiction.

NICOLE MARIE WILLIAMS is entering her third year of graduate study at the University of California, Santa Barbara. She has a B.A. and a Secondary Teaching Credential from Brown University and an M.A. from UCSB. She teaches junior and senior high school English and history at Faith Academy in Santa Barbara.